Under My Elm

Books by
DAVID GRAYSON

Under My Elm

The Countryman's Year

Adventures in Solitude

A Day of Pleasant Bread

Adventures in Contentment

Adventures in Friendship

Adventures in Understanding

Great Possessions

Hempfield

The Friendly Road

DAVID GRAYSON

Under My Elm

COUNTRY DISCOVERIES AND REFLECTIONS

Illustrated by
DAVID HENDRICKSON

 RENAISSANCE
HOUSE

A Division of Jende-Hagan, Inc.
541 Oak Street • P.O. Box 177
Frederick, CO 80530

RENAISSANCE HOUSE PUBLISHERS
A Division of Jende-Hagan, Inc.
541 Oak Street • P.O. Box 177
Frederick, CO   80530

Library of Congress Cataloging in Publication Data

Baker, Ray Stannard, 1870-1946.
    Under my elm.

    Reprint. Originally published: Garden City,
N.Y. : Doubleday, Doran, 1942.
    1. Baker, Ray Stannard, 1870-1946—Biography.
2. Authors, American—20th century—Biography.
3. Country life—Massachusetts. I. Title.
PS3503.A5448U5   1986   818'.5203   [B]   86-24819
ISBN 0-939650-47-9

CONTENTS

		PAGE
	INTRODUCTION	vii
I	LIFE ON THE LAND	3
II	MY BEES	19
III	A DAY OF HIGH ADVENTURE	35
IV	A FELLOWSHIP OF CURIOSITY	53
V	ONION FIELD	77
VI	LIVING IN A TROUBLED WORLD	117
VII	MY ELM TREE	135
VIII	BIRDS I HAVE KNOWN	151
IX	WE GO FISHING	165
X	THINGS I DELIGHT IN	177
XI	A CHRONICLE OF SMALL JOYS	185
XII	COMMENTARIES	195
XIII	SAYINGS TO LIVE BY	203
XIV	A CAPTIVITY ENRICHED	219
XV	THE LAST THING OF ALL	277

For every man truly lives, so long as he acts his nature, or some way makes good the faculties of himself. RELIGIO MEDICI

Under My Elm

MEN are commonly unhappy who do not know how to act their own natures or truly make good the faculties of themselves.

It was on an October day, year before last, that this conclusion of a busy life came powerfully upon me and I thought first of writing this book. I had been hard at work, picking and bringing in the last of the Baldwin apples, storing them safe in the apple cellar. I was returning to the orchard with my baskets, trundling the empty wheelbarrow. I passed the tall walnut trees, from which many of the nuts had already fallen. I stopped a moment near the busy hives. It was a golden autumn day.

As I stood there by the hives, it came to me suddenly and with strange intensity that I might not be here many years longer, among the things I love, and that I had not begun to write of all the things I had seen and heard and felt and thought since I came here to this hillside. All that life here has meant to me! If it were money and land I had, I could leave them without remorse, since they would go on working equally well for other people. I need not concern myself about that. But a man's thoughts, his ripe experience, the treasures of his knowledge, what he has gained in all his years of wisdom, or of beauty, or of friendship perish with him unless he has communicated them, in one way or another, before he dies.

This was no new thought, but it had never come to me before with greater poignancy of power and feeling; I stood there thinking, with an intensification of life such as I have rarely known.

I thought of all that had happened in the thirty years and more since I came here to this earth with my emptiness and was filled; for it was long after I learned how to work that I learned how to live. I thought of the hard-driven earlier years before I had discovered what it was that I needed to do and how I was to do it. I remembered the very day when I came walking down into the back pasture of old Brigham's farm and sat down in the rowen, not far from the place where our house now stands. There was then no road that came into it: I had to climb two fences. I looked across the wide valley to Mt. Warner and beyond that, a little to the south, to the Holyoke Range and the more distant Berkshire Hills. It was at this very time of year, in October, with still sunshine and an autumn haze upon the hills.

INTRODUCTION

I sat there a long time looking at the distant farmsteads, the comfortable pastures in which cattle were peacefully feeding, and the farmhouses and barns half hidden among the trees. One great silo rose like a tower out of Colomont farm; and beyond that, a spire or two in the haze, lay the town of Northampton.

I felt suddenly a love of that place, a longing to remain just there for all my days.

My dream of that October day came true. We bought the back fields of old Brigham's farm. We laid out a road into it that finally became a street in the town, we built our home upon the hillside. It seems strange, looking back, that once we began to do what we really needed to do, so many fortunate things happened to help us.

Here on this hillside in Amherst we have lived ever since, now more than thirty years. We have been happy here. Here our children grew up; and we have lived to see their children coming every summer to play in our orchard and romp down through our pasture. Looking back, at the age of seventy, I recall much hard work, I recall discouragements and disappointments, I recall inevitable sorrow, but I have never once in all that time regretted that we gave up something of the world in order to know something more of the earth. We have found here the place where we were best fitted to live and to work.

INTRODUCTION

This book contains an account of many of the things that have happened here: much that we have seen and heard, much that we have thought and felt.

DAVID GRAYSON

FOREWORD TO THE
RENAISSANCE HOUSE EDITION

If one believed in reincarnation (which I do not), one would quickly conclude that David Grayson, author of *Under My Elm,* was somehow compelled by some other inner spirit to "be fruitful and multiply." Here is a perfectly productive writer who, for thirty years, toiled over ten acres of land in the Connecticut Valley near Amherst, Massachusetts, with nothing to show for it in any monetary sense, stung by his bees and working "like a slave" to get the witch grass out of the old fields.

Nothing to show for it! The author quotes Goethe: "Agriculture is a very fine thing because you get such an unmistakable answer as to whether you're making a fool of yourself or hitting the mark." And the author clearly hits the mark in recounting his love affair with his ten barren acres which he and his family transformed into a virtual cornucopia of flowering trees, grapevines, gardens of all sorts, and beehives overlooking the valley from the backside of Brigham's farm in Amherst. At age seventy, Grayson realizes that while he can will the land and the house to someone, he cannot pass along the story of how it came to be without pausing to write it all down.

Anyone who is in tune with the land and its cycles will be enriched by Grayson's story, especially his experience over time with his bees. He has to learn slowness (otherwise they bite); and he makes friends in an English vicarage with a fellow beekeeper who has "the answer!"

Why he titles the book *Under My Elm* with some emphasis on MY, when in fact the elm in question belongs to someone else, is curious but not too disturbing, for Grayson is not growing for profit, but for love. Hard physical work in the field, laborious and repetitive, seems to awaken in him an awareness of the interrelation of bird to bee to tree to flower and of him to them.

In New England there are not many "fruitful" farming locations. I used to pass up old Route 5 on the way to my home in Dublin, New Hampshire, and I always marvelled at the tobacco farms in the Connecticut River valley. I know exactly where Grayson lives; you cannot see Northampton and Mt. Warner and the Holyoke range at one sitting in Amherst without being approximately in one location. One always wonders how the early settlers raised enough to keep themselves through the winter, but Grayson clearly shows that, with patience and an ear tuned to nature's ways, the land will provide; it is only man who fails.

Grayson falls ill and, in a late chapter, explains his battle with pain, powerful pain. It is almost a separate book, but by that time we have grown so fond of the author, we hope he can be relieved to go back to his beloved acres in Amherst. Thirty years in one place is a rarity these days; Grayson has shown he is persistent. He will win the battle.

--Rob Trowbridge, Publisher
Yankee Magazine
Dublin, N.H.
June, 1986

RAY STANNARD BAKER (DAVID GRAYSON)
1870-1946

Wrote Ray Stannard Baker on the birth of David Grayson:
"On the whole...I was gloomy about the project; but I was heartened by a letter I soon received, written by Lincoln Steffans, an editor and a friend. It was certainly one of the finest appreciations that ever I received in my life. It was then, and has remained, one of those creative documents in a man's life which give him courage to go on:"

July 25, 1906

My Dear Baker:
Your David Grayson...is beautiful...I was ashamed because I never had realized that there was in you such a sense of beauty, so much fine, philosophic wisdom and, most wonderful of all—serenity...It's a real creative art, Baker, far above and beyond reporting... David Grayson is a great man...

THE GRAYSON ELM

David Grayson's elm, as it appeared in 1912, near his Amherst, Massachusetts home. When Mr. Baker (Grayson) heard of a farmer's plan to fell the tree because it shaded his corn field, he bought the lot to protect it. The great tree has since been saved from Dutch Elm disease and is, today, in the care of the Amherst Garden Club, where it has some voice in town meetings. The Baker home is now the Delta Chi fraternity house and Sunset Avenue is a busy street, separating the tree from the house.

(Photo provided by Baker's daughter-in-law, Mrs. Roger D. Baker)

Life on the Land

I

Life on the Land

MY DREAM, in the beginning, was of a few acres with hills not far off, a field or pasture, an orchard, a garden—a possible cow, a pig or so, chickens and turkeys. I did not think of beekeeping, which gave me finally so much satisfaction, until later. I wanted a place not too big, where I could work with my own hands and yet keep on with my profession, which was that of a busy writer. I longed to live on the land, get deeply acquainted with it, somehow get it into me.

I hoped, and actually calculated, that we could raise enough on eight or ten acres to furnish a considerable part of our subsistence, as indeed we actually did at a later time, with enough surplus *perhaps* to pay the taxes and other expenses—which never quite happened. I remember, one year, having what I considered a wonderful crop of cabbages; I remember also the shock I had when I tried to sell it.

"How many tons have you got?" asked the cold-eyed dealer.

Tons! I found I was competing with market-gardeners who produced everything by machinery. I managed to sell part of my crop to local merchants, and we thriftily ate cabbages all winter. I dug them out of the pits when there was a foot or more of snow on the ground.

I knew well enough that any such experiment in living must represent all sorts of compromises—what life is not a compromise?—but it was truly what I had dreamed about, what I longed for, and what I had finally attained. Our land had to be near a town, where there were schools. Our home had not only to meet the requirements of a large family, it was also, necessarily, the home of a writer as well as of a farmer. And all along, for years, with the continual struggle for supremacy between pen and plow, I had constantly to adjust my daily employment.

In order to find quiet and escape interruption, I was often up at dawn, four or five o'clock, on warm summer mornings. I had a table on the wide west porch where I could, whenever I lifted my eyes, look off across the valley to the hills. I made good progress with my writing for an hour or so, and then the country began to come alive around me. The sun rose higher, the grass put on its spangles of morning dew, and all at once the countryside seemed to awaken gloriously—the birds were singing, the dogs exchanging morning greetings across the fields, the cows lowing, eager to be milked and turned out to pasture, and all the henyards in the neighborhood had become suddenly garrulous.

For some time, by sheer determination, I could keep my pen going—even though I might feel like whistling or singing with the best of them.

One temptation I could never resist. I sat where I could look out over my beehives, and when, sometime in the warm forenoon, I heard the roar of a swarm rising in the sunny air, I stopped even in the middle of a sentence and ran down to see which colony it was coming from. After that, of course, I had to look up often to make sure where it was lighting, in what apple tree or on what currant bush, and presently, with what a rush of pleasure, I threw my pen aside and went out with my hive tools and with veil and gloves to cut down the great brown swarm and rehive it. All these things, of course, interrupted me. I failed always to do as much writing as I had intended or hoped—I could never satisfy the voracious editors!—and yet I never came back to my work on the porch, or in my study, without a fresh sense of the wonder and the beauty of life—a new appreciation that I was a humble part of it all, and that it was infinitely desirable. I never spent such a morning as this without resolving never again to be dogmatic about anything in this world; I began to learn that life, after all, was first, and writing second.

We were all more or less ignorant of farming and gardening in New England, but from the grandfather, who lived with us and was in many ways the best of us, down to the children of the family, we were all eager to have a hand in the new enterprise. We tried all sorts of experiments. We got acquainted with our knowing neighbors—there are few better ways to make a friendship, or cement it, than by asking advice—and even when we discovered a confusion of wisdom as to weather and wind and soil and seed, we learned much as to what to do. Every spring we studied innumerable seed and nursery catalogues; we joined a farmers' club, where we enjoyed the Yankee wit and the Yankee stories even more than the sober discussions we heard. Every spring we had so many new ideas that we uprooted or rearranged a considerable proportion of the plantings we had made the year before.

Since we had a clean slate to write upon, we could do whatever we liked. When we bought our land, it was an open field that had been cultivated probably for a hundred years. Save for one great maple tree in the lower pasture (now more than four feet in diameter), it was as bare of any planting as an Arizona desert. Today there are two huge white ash trees near our house; they are nearly two feet in diameter, and some fifty high. We set out these trees with our own hands, when they were mere whip saplings dug out of a neighboring wood lot. We have a wonderful beech tree with branches that spread over thirty feet, several noble pin oaks, and huge pines and spruces that have made for themselves a miniature bit of forest carpeted with brown pine needles. We can now sit in the shade of them on hot summer days, and they fend off the chilly blasts of winter. Our grandchildren build secret tree houses among their leafy fastnesses and swing from their stout branches. What a miracle—all in thirty years!

Every tree, every shrub, every berry bush and perennial around the house and in the garden, we planted. We have lived with them through many summers and winters; we have cared for them, pruned and cultivated and fertilized them with our own hands. We know them personally and intimately: all of their little individual excellences and beauties, their limitations and waywardnesses—and we love them. Some may think that these common things are not riches; so may people have riches all around them that they never see.

Sometimes in later years, since I have not been able to work as much as I should like with my own hands, I have had much pleasure in walking down through the garden and orchard, counting up the treasures we have created there. No poet reading his own precious verses, after he has ceased writing verses, has had more joy than I have had in watching the apples and pears and peaches ripen on our trees, and the raspberries come red, and the blackberries black, on our bushes—and the grapes in September hanging heavy upon our trellises. The other day, in my pride, I made a list of all the trees and berry bushes we now have:

Eleven apple trees, several large old ones in full bearing; the others, planted to take the place of those destroyed in the hurricane of 1938, are not yet full-grown. We have had the best luck with the old dependable New England apple, the Baldwin; the McIntosh and Gravenstein, which are best worth eating out of hand, also do well by us.

Twelve peach trees, mostly Belle of Georgia, which are eccentric producers. I have replanted them about once in five years.

Three fine old pear trees, two Bartletts and a Clapp, which require almost no attention, live a long time, and produce a large crop every year.

Three young plum trees which we planted to take the place of several large old ones that bore prodigiously for a few years and died finally of the cancerous black knot.

Four fine nut trees, two black walnut, a Siberian walnut, and a butternut, three of them in bearing. Some years back we had a beautiful English walnut tree, nearly forty feet tall, which had begun to yield plentifully and of which I was inordinately proud, since everyone had told me that our winters were too cold for English walnuts. Pride goeth before a fall: the frosts of 1935 laid it low!

We have besides these trees several lesser fruit crops: three beds of raspberries—the best, the Latham—which yield steadily and plentifully, even though we have had to fight the mosaic disease. Besides having all the berries we can eat during the weeks of their fruitage, nearly every year, what raspberry jam have we enjoyed all winter long! We have blackberries, which insist on spreading in every direction and are more or less a thorny nuisance, and many varieties of grapes. We tried hopefully, some years ago, to raise cultivated blue-berries, but our soil was not sour enough, and the gray squirrels got most of the berries before they were ripe.

Our field crops presented more serious difficulties. As I have said, we tried many experiments. Onions and tobacco, both highly specialized and hazardous crops, are the principal cash products of our valley. I did not dare aspire to either for several years, but satisfied my-self with humdrum crops of potatoes and corn—both of which taught me much that I needed to know. I did not at first realize the truth of the remark of one of my pungent neighbors:

"There's a hell of a lot of work in eight acres of potatoes!"

He said the same thing even more emphatically years later when I began to experiment with onion growing, as I shall presently relate.

We learned also, and somewhat expensively, what it takes to "bring up" an old field that has been cultivated, not too well, for a century or more. It had looked deceptively smooth and green and beautiful that first spring: we were to discover that it was infested with witch grass—also called quack grass—one of the worst of all the farmer's enemies—and in the lower part, much narrow-leaf dock, a great, coarse, tough weed with a tenacious rootage which is supposed to be thoroughly killed only when placed in the public road where wagons and horses and automobiles can run over it for a month or so. We fought both of these marauders vigorously and steadily, and finally cleared our land entirely of them.

The lower part of the land, where it slid away toward the marsh, was wet, and one spring we laid drains all the way down the hill, hundreds of feet of them, with many branch lines. I staked out the levels myself— with delight—and did no inconsiderable part of the digging of the ditches and the laying of the tile with my own hands—this with much less delight, but with an earned appetite every day for dinner such as I had not known before in many years.

I know from experience, and an aching back, exactly how such jobs as these are done. In the beginning, what I wanted most was hand work, actual experience of the land. I did not pretend to be a "practical farmer," nor yet an "agriculturist," as one of my sly neighbors called me with a glint in his eye. I needed to know what digging was like, and chopping, and plowing and planting and fertilizing and cultivating; and when a man really wants good hard, hand labor—I have found—nobody is going to prevent him from getting it.

I began the fight immediately, without regard to the importance of the task I selected or the energy I applied to it. The enemies were there, and I smote them. The land drains and the narrow-leaf dock and the witch grass! I find entries in my notebooks regarding these early struggles, which, if they record no immediate profit from my strenuous labor, reveal how earnest I was in going at it. This was written on June 9:

Again in the meadow yesterday, digging at the marsh ditch not far from the northern line of our land. It was wet, a fine mist in the air, and the grass was high and heavy. I had to take a spade to loosen up each square of sod before I could get down into the soil. It was hard work. I came in soaked to the skin, every garment dripping, but I enjoyed it.

I enjoyed everything about it. A great many meadow larks and bobolinks were in the fields. I flushed a covey of quail that sailed over the fence into the marsh, and I saw many swallows, robins, and sparrows. They gave me good company. The clover and alfalfa in my field are heavy, but the other grasses, except meadow fescue, are not so good.

I don't know what it is, but there is something about steady manual labor like this, alone in the fields, that gives one a curious deep satisfaction. I like the sense of doing hard work that is also useful work. One's mind at first drops asleep, except for the narrow margin relating to this or that repetitive process. One lets go, calms down. For hours, sometimes, while at such work, I came near the point of complete mental vacuity. The mind sets itself the minute task it has to do and goes off somewhere to its own high pastures, serene uplands, to rest and play. The hours pass magically: the sun that was low when the work began rides high in the heavens—and suddenly the mind comes home again. It comes home refreshed, stimulated, happy. I always know the exact moment of its arrival. Yesterday it did not return until I had nearly finished my work in the field. It seemed to cry out: "What, asleep! Listen to the bobolinks."

I straightened up quickly and realized that I had been working for several hours without hearing or seeing much of anything—this literally. The whole world now became flooded with delightful sounds, not only the bobolinks, but a hundred other voices both of nature and human nature, so that I had a deep and indescribably friendly feeling toward all things. I thought it good and beautiful to be there and to be alive. Even the grass clinging wetly to my legs as I walked seemed consciously holding me close to the earth; and the shovel held warmly, even painfully in my blistered hands, was proof that I had at last become part of a universal process. These sensations, even as I set them down, seem difficult to express, but they were *there,* and they were true and sound.

I find that many of my notes, made at that time, express my eagerness, yes, my passion, to get close to the earth, to take hold of it in every possible way, to know it, to feel it. I find this record of certain of my experiences at that time:

When we speak of a meadow, we think only of the top of the forest of the grass—the waving branches and leaves;

but this is only a suggestion of the deeper mystery. I took pains yesterday to examine more closely a space about ten feet square which, fifty feet away, would seem to be a clean hay field of herd's-grass, redtop, and clover. I looked down deep into the mysterious minute world one so rarely sees— the primeval forest of the grass. I was astonished at the teeming variety of life I found there when I went down on my knees, as one must do when he goes to nature. The carpeted earth was covered with lichens and moss and a score of small shade-grown plants, the existence of which I could not have imagined. Besides the clover and the fodder grasses, I found two kinds of minute ferns, sorrel, buttercup, one innocently small plant of rascally narrow-leaf dock, dandelions, smartweed, wild carrot (which, in blossoming, is known as Queen Anne's lace), and at least three varieties of moss. Besides these more or less common plants, I counted several large and small growths, the names of which, being no botanist, I do not know. This is not a weedy meadow either, as meadows here go, and will bear this summer a fair crop of hay.

I found also that this small spot of the teeming earth had a geography and topography of its own. It had its miniature hills and valleys, its rolling plains. There is even a lake (when it rains) as big as the hoof of a horse; and two small field stones for hills.

I took to imagining myself suddenly reduced in size to a hop-o'-my-thumb explorer in this vast forest, crossing the Africa of wilderness between the orchard and the edge of the cornfield. I marveled at the enormous prehistoric animals I saw clinging like sloths to the branches of some of the larger trees (slugs, you know) and would have shot at them with my trusty rifle if I had had one. Here and there great serpents thrust their heads out of the earth (they looked like the angleworms of another world), and there were strange and fearsome creatures flying through the air or hiding among the foliage—a beetle as big as an elephant and a spider that looked like an eagle.

I knelt there fascinated for an hour or more, and came away thinking how we go blindly about our dull tasks, our eyes and ears and nose closed to the wonders of the world, not knowing where to turn for joy.

So often these absorbing early observations led me to comments and reflections which I find now in my notebooks. Here is one that relates to the incident I have just set down:

Suppose that hop-o'-my-thumb explorer of the forest of the grass were to see *Me* as I really am, or guess at me, or predicate me, towering above him there to the skies: I wonder if he would think me a god, or God? I should possess for him, indeed, the power of life and death. A single crude footstep might destroy him and his whole world. I could change his whole environment with a share of a plow, or a handful of new seeds, or a pinch or two of fertilizer.

I found myself delighted with these imaginings, following them up for several days with additional speculations:

There is this about the Maker, whoever and whatever He may be: He never scamps a job. He works as well and as truly in a ten-foot plot as in a continent. There is as much beauty and perfection—and indeed mystery—under my hand as I rest it down here in the grass as in the broad sweep of the Connecticut Valley. Underneath and within, it is as complete, as workable, as it is overhead and outside. So many sights, so many minute mysteries I cannot see; so many sounds I cannot hear; I think I shall never reach the end of the wonders.

I began to love that hillside in Amherst. I left it always with regret; I returned to it with joy. I find in my notebooks many expressions of this strong feeling. Here is one I wrote on a Sunday morning in March:

I came home by the night train, sleeping ill. As I walked down Amity Street in the still morning, with the sunshine warm among the bare elms and little rivulets of water from the heaped snow running in the walks, I came suddenly alive with a curious joy. Dear, quiet town! I looked out through the vista at the end of the road to the western hills, now soft with the faint blue haze of the wintry morning, and something hard, strained, worried within me began to unknit. My own hills! I looked at the friendly homes as I passed, and thought of all the people within I knew so well. I thought of the lives—the joyful, tragic, sorrowful lives going on all about, and I so near to see and know, and it seemed as though I could never again leave these streets, this little town.

I have been where there was too much talk, too many *things*, food more than I needed, amusement keyed too high; where speed and not beauty seemed the test of life; and I come home again to my own calm hills, my own town, to the beautiful quiet of my own thoughts. If only people would be still for a little and look at the world before they drown everything in torrents of talk! If they would only be

satisfied without rushing through life at sixty miles an hour
—and dreaming of a hundred and twenty! If they would
only stop for a day or so and love people before trying to
reform them!

I am at home again! Dear, quiet Amherst: the wide
valley, the hills, and the little town. The tall bare elms of
the shaded streets, the morning sun warm upon one's
shoulder blades, the crows calling across the snowy fields,
and the smoke of friendly breakfast fires rising through the
still morning air.

I am at home again.

My Bees

II

My Bees

IT WAS NOT until several years after we came to Amherst that I discovered the kind of country work that suited me best. In fact, it suited me exactly and completely, for I found in it unending interest and variety. This was beekeeping and all that went with it in human contacts of various sorts and in exploring the astonishingly voluminous lore and literature of the honeybee. In time I came to take pride in the quality of the honey I sold. I liked to see the little pyramid of my jars with their translucent contents in Dickinson's Store, with the sign which the energetic grocer put below it: DAVID GRAYSON'S GOOD HONEY.

It was in its way as enjoyable as seeing my name on the title page of a new book.

I recall the pleasure I felt one day when a visitor came ambling down through my garden and inquired:

"Are you the feller that keeps bees?"

I felt that I had truly become a member of the fraternity: I was accepted as a professional.

Beekeeping had another decided advantage for a man of my profession, which I soon recognized. During the winter months, when I was busiest with my writing, when I had oftenest to be away from home, the bees were safely lodged in their winter quarters—from November until April—and required little or no attention.

I was a slow learner, and for a strange reason: I was too quick. I was too intense. I had learned in cities, and thought it a virtue to hurry. I wanted my successes immediately, by Wednesday afternoon.

But nature is incurably deliberate: it does not hurry, it takes time to grow. It awaits its seasons, it is as content with its Aprils as with its Augusts; with its evenings as with its golden dawns. Its finest products are not the result of the strenuous haste that men cultivate, but of the slow unfolding of creative processes.

My best teachers in this new learning, so valuable to me through the years, were my bees. There is no hurrying a hive of bees. The first law of the beemaster is to go slow and be steady, and the penalty for disobedience is prompt and pointed. One gets stung! I know of few other processes in nature where the reaction is more immediate and instructive.

I was stung. I was stung again. Even when I was well armored with veil and long canvas gloves I was stung. For I was clumsily disrespectful of the highly developed social manners and communal habits of the bees—a huge, crude, ill-mannered outsider bursting in upon a well and gently ordered commonwealth. I jarred the citizens of that society out of their tranquillity in getting the frames out of or into the busy hives: I often injured them, and sometimes even killed a few of them, even if unwittingly. My ear had not yet become attuned to the more delicate and courteous warnings of coming trouble, which I learned later to recognize.

In going to nature, we are so often obtuse, so often arrogant, so little humble, that we do not listen and look for the shy, deep things that are so often the most significant. We bring back only what we took with us —our own selfish absorptions and humdrum interests and moralities. There is a harmony in nature, if we can come to hear it, and a rhythm, if we can learn to adapt ourselves to it, that will give us a strange and blessed new tranquillity of soul.

I learned gradually the beautiful art of the beemaster. When I sat down of a morning in the sunshine beside a hive, I always paused for a moment to watch the swift coming and going of its busy inhabitants. It told me of the present humor of the bees and it was in itself such a harmonious expression of happy labor that I liked to watch it for itself. I began soon to feel myself growing calm and steady. When I opened the hive, I did it slowly. I took time for each separate motion. I was careful not to jar the hive or to break too suddenly the propolis that holds down the cover board, and I went slowly, slowly, at the business of loosening the frames and easing them out of the hive. I watched the bees themselves, all the little suspicious or angry excursions that the watchers make in time of danger; and I listened for the unmistakable change in the humming contentment of the hive, which indicates that the bees are becoming irritated. There are times when the trouble is with the weather, a muggy day or a cold or rainy one, when bee sensibilities, like human sensibilities, are touchy. Whatever the cause, there is a point when the beemaster would better put aside his hive tool, turn out the smudge in his smoker, fold up his veil, and go home.

I have known the time when a colony, though smoked thoroughly and apparently handled with care, would suddenly rise out of the hive and attack the invader en masse. At such a time the best of veils, gloves, thick clothing will not entirely keep them out. Their lives are nothing. Every bee that stings dies, but what of that! I have known of horses that inadvertently disturbed a colony or overturned a hive to be literally stung to death. Men have been stung to death. Though immensely larger, stronger, than the bees, the master does well not to be too rough or go too far. He may argue that it is he who owns and orders the hives, feeds them during winters, when their own stores are not sufficient—nevertheless, there comes a time, unless he be indeed a wise beemaster, when the colony will have none of him, when it will sacrifice, wholesale, its lives, destroy utterly its own orderly organization—but it will be free! But it will live its own life according to its own genius!

I sometimes think how much the statesman might learn, from a year or so of beekeeping, of the respect for cultures different from his own—the bees had a civilization for thousands of years before man was man at all—and by practicing the courtesy due them, the consideration, the patience, help both them and himself. The other day I read a graphic paper on what is now happening in Europe. I should hate to be the master of that hive! Four or five hundred million restless Europeans! Put out your smokers now, wise Germans, lay aside your sharp tools, your armor you may as well fold up—the colony is aroused. Life, order, health, organization are nothing!—they will be free of you. Strong as you are, great as you have been, they may sting you to death. Look out, Adolf Hitler!

In time I began to learn *slowness*. "Slowness," as Rodin says in a remark I have often quoted, "slowness is beauty." I learned courtesy, and a kind of observant humility, so that for years I have scarcely been stung at all. I have at times experimented with handling my bees without veil or gloves—but rarely without a smoker —for I know now when and how to do it. As soon as I had begun to understand the laws of the hive, the bees and I worked well together.

Since I began, now many years ago, to write a little

here and there about beekeeping, especially in my book
called *The Countryman's Year*, I have had many letters
from people who wanted to know more about the art or
thought of practicing it. My advice has always been,
"Go slow." Begin with one colony and learn the habits
of the bees and the art of handling them. They multiply
all too rapidly, and the problem of the beginner is often
to keep from having too many colonies. A good queen
in the highly productive years of her life will lay hundreds of eggs a day.

The error of so many people who go to the land, unless they have had previous experience, is to attempt
too much at first. Having worked out their plans on
paper, they expect productive results, especially in cash
returns, too soon. As I have said, the practice of the
city, the tempo of its feverish activity, cannot be applied
to the land. And profit in cash can never be made the
chief test of the satisfactions of life in the country—at
least to the part-time farmer. I went off the money
standard long ago.

A man can soon find out whether he likes beekeeping, or any other farm operation, and whether he is well
adapted to it. If he finds he is not, he had better stop
at once.

I know country beekeepers who are contemptuous of
"book learnin' "; they are usually poor beemen. I have
always got everything I could out of books, but never
relied wholly upon what I found in them. I have always

wanted to test a recommended process for myself before adopting it for my daily uses. In fact, I have enjoyed many a hot controversy with pontifical bee authorities, and since I never had time to let any of them know about my objections, I always came out ahead.

The earliest book I used seems to me still an excellent one for beginners. It is called *How to Keep Bees,* by Anna B. Comstock. *Bees for the Beginner,* a new bulletin issued free by the United States Department of Agriculture, is also most useful. As one gets deeper into the art, he will wish to have that vast compendium, nearly a thousand pages, full of more or less unassorted and sometimes repetitive information, called *The A B C and X Y Z of Beekeeping.* It is edited by the most famous of American bee families, the Roots, of Medina, Ohio.

I have no intention of making this in any wise a treatise on beekeeping, for there are plenty of better books on the mechanics of the art than I could possibly write. What I wish to do is to tell of some of the rich rewards, besides honey, that have come to me.

I remember some of my early embarrassed attempts to market my honey. I knew well enough how to sell the stories and essays and books I wrote, but when I went to town with a box or basket of my honey, I was in a new and unfamiliar world. I was suspect: a writer daring to compete with professional beekeepers! On one of those early occasions I walked homeward considerably discouraged. My basket was indeed empty; I had sold my honey. I knew it was a first-class product, every section well filled and capped, and the comb as white and clean as any bees ever made. But when I held out the money I had received for it in the palm of my hand, my heart went down. I remember sitting down by the roadside to make some figures as to profits and losses. It soon appeared, even when I made allowances for being a beginner, that every comb of my honey had cost me far more than the shrewd-eyed merchant had paid me—and this without making any adequate allowance for my own labor.

"At this rate," I said to myself, "I shall soon be an agricultural pauper."

I began to feel pretty blue, and yet somehow not satisfied that the calculations I had made were wholly correct. I could not look back upon the experiences I had had without a real sense of reward. I began to think of the quiet joy I had known, the long hours working at the minute pleasurable tasks of the apiary in the bee corner of my basement, where I keep my tools and supplies. I thought how often I had come from my work and thrown aside my bee veil and gloves with a sense of refreshment impossible to describe. So it was that, as I walked homeward swinging my empty basket, I began to be more and more confident, even quite happy. What if I didn't make a cash profit the first year or so? I had *lived:* I had lived more interestingly, and in some ways, perhaps more usefully (producing good honey as well as uncertainly good manuscripts), than ever before in my life. With that I began, with delight, to work out an accounting of my transactions on a new basis, writing down the items as I walked, with a stubby pencil in my pocket account book:

Honey, first three lots, cost to produce, about	$26.00	
Honey, received for three lots, cash and trade		12.00
Joy at the job since April, 6 mos. @ $3.00		18.00
First-class appetite for supper every night for 6 mos. @ $1.00		6.00
Comfortable weariness and good sound sleep after hard labor out-of-doors during same period @ $1.00		6.00
Interesting and inventive thoughts. (Capitalists have long considered experimental inventions a valuable asset. Why not I, inventions of the imagination?) 6 mos. @ $3.00		18.00
Good will. This item appears in many sound accountings of great companies. Why not in mine? I've already earned the good will of several people in this neighborhood. More than that, I've earned more of my own good will than ever before, I think, in a like period. So in it goes.		1.00
Balance—clear profit	35.00	
	$61.00	$61.00

I reached home soon afterwards feeling like a millionaire. Oh, I was cocky! As I figured it out, I had made something over 135 per cent on my first three lots of honey. That's business, I said. Very few industries I know can match it—especially in times like these, when there seems to be too much of everything.

"But," I said to myself, "I haven't heard of anyone yet who has too much of my best products—too much appetite, say for supper, especially if it comes of hard work out-of-doors, or too cheerful a spirit, or too many inventions of a free and easy mind."

"Depression!" I said, "there is no depression around here."

When I showed my calculations to my Mentor, she looked at me with an appraising and skeptical eye and was far more eloquent in her comments for saying nothing at all. In all the years I have known her, she has been good for me! She keeps me down, where I belong, upon the earth.

While these comforting reflections pleased me, I knew perfectly well that the business of beekeeping, as of growing potatoes, onions, corn, and cabbages, was as real as their production; and I determined that sooner or later I'd also make a *money* profit on my work and get all the other rewards thrown in. I was as covetous and grasping as that!

The great mistake that I made in the first place—that all amateurs make—was in underestimating the knowledge and skill required in making a success of even the simpler processes of the land. So many men think that they are going down in the scale of life, or going back, when they return to what they call the "simple life" of the country. They will soon find that their country neighbors, whether Yankee or Polish stock, as in this valley, have stores of knowledge and experience never dreamed of in their philosophies or taught in their schools. I could write pages on the when, the where, the how, and the what of applying fertilizer on our peculiar valley soils—learned through many years, mostly from Polish friends of mine. The same is true of plowing and planting and harvesting. A man may, indeed, live on a farm without being a farmer; but if he expects to get results in good crops, he must work at it as hard—harder!—as at most other callings.

And of all the country arts, few are more complicated —if one really demands a profit from it—than beekeeping. So many things turn upon the weather, the kind and quality of nectar- and pollen-bearing flowers that nature, in her careless abundance, is willing to produce; when the honey flow begins, and how long it lasts. The beemaster must know how to handle his colonies in the spring, so that they will be boiling full of bees just when the honey flow begins. He must be sure of strong young queens, he must learn to control swarming (always a difficult business), so that the bees will devote most of their strength, not so much to producing more bees, as more honey. He must put on his supers at the right moment, he must be constantly fighting insect and bird and animal (and small boy) pests. He must know when and how to take off his product, how to extract it, how to process it, how to pack it, and finally how to sell it. I could easily see that my early disappointments were due to no defect in the art but to my own practice of it.

I began presently to keep a card catalogue of my colonies, setting forth the condition in each hive as I went through it, so that I knew always what was going on in every hive, whether the queen was laying vigorously, how much drone brood was developing, whether or not the bees were working in the comb-honey supers, and many other facts—all indispensable knowledge if one is to have profitable surpluses of honey.

I did not, of course, devote my whole time to the work—else I might have learned more rapidly—and there were unavoidable absences from home, so that it was only after twelve or fifteen years' experience that I began to get really good results. One summer the white clover blossoms were unusually abundant, and I had a wonderful crop of honey. Since I had been keeping a careful account of my receipts and expenditures, I was able to make out an accounting that pleased me very much indeed. I was so vainglorious that I even delved into the yearly balance sheets of several great American corporations to see what profits they had made, in comparison with mine. So far as the percentages were concerned, I found I had beaten the United States Steel Corporation all hollow! I had beaten still more disastrously the New York Central Railroad. I had even beaten one of the greatest gold mining enterprises in the world—the Homestake. I am speaking, of course, of the percentage of my profit on capital actually invested—compared with the profits made by those leviathans on their capital. And I am not leaving out a good allowance for my own labor. One year I made enough profit—*profit*, mind you!—to pay for my entire outfit, and I had enough honey left over for pancakes all winter.

After making these calculations, I felt like going about with my thumbs in the armholes of my vest! When I showed my "financial statement," as I called it, to my Mentor, she looked at me with a kind of indulgent comprehension.

"You are utterly incorrigible," said she.

I almost forgot to speak of another important consideration, if beekeeping is to remain an exciting, as well as profitable, calling. So many men I know, not beekeepers alone, have lost all joy in their work: every thought, every effort, is devoted to a harassing pursuit of a larger income. In my case, with all my other interests and problems, I found I could manage ten or a dozen colonies of bees and enjoy them thoroughly;

when I got more, I began to find them a burden. I could no longer do the work with my own hands: I had the sense of being driven. I found this true also of other branches of my small farming and gardening operations. If I had too many apple trees and grapevines, I could not do all the pruning myself and have things the way I wanted them. And as I looked about me, I found that even in our free country—which is a well-known paradise!—I observed there were still many slaves—slaves to cows and pigs, slaves to onions and tobacco, even slaves to the honeybee. I was somewhat comforted to find that there were also slaves in stores and banks and plumbers' establishments! But while a pig-slave can eat his pork with enjoyment, and a potato-slave his potatoes, who ever heard of a bondholder nibbling his coupons?

I should say that one of the marks of a truly sensible man is that he can draw the hair-fine line between joy and profit. I can often pick out such a man by the look in his eye.

A Day of High Adventure

III

A Day of High Adventure

IT WAS QUITE a number of years after I began bee-keeping, and had learned to love all its interesting and intricate processes, that I discovered, or began to discover, what a world-wide humming the honeybee has made all down through the years of recorded history. I found it in literature and philosophy, I found it in the arts and sciences. After a time I began to note references to bees and beekeeping in every book I read. It was like discovering the name of a dear friend acclaimed for his wisdom by bigwig statesmen or commended by studious critics. I soon began to mark and sometimes to copy down such references, and the more I found, the more the wonder grew. I began to think the honeybee quite a fellow!

One of the earliest references to set me going—and make me combative!—I found in a casual rereading of Carlyle's *Sartor Resartus*. It was in Chapter III:

"Bees will not work except in darkness; Thought will not work except in Silence: neither will Virtue work except in Secrecy."

"That," said I, when I had read it a second time, "is assuredly one of the worst similes that ever I saw in my life."

I have always liked crusty old Thomas Carlyle, with the soul of him so full of poetry, but this irritated me. Just at that time I was experimenting with a glass hive that I had set up in my study, with a little hole through the window frame for the bees to get in and out. It was a southern window with full exposure to the sunshine, and even as I read Carlyle's words I could look up and see the bees working as industriously as though they were in the customary darkness of their hives. I wished my poet and moralist had known his bees before hanging such a weight of philosophical homily upon their supposed characteristics. For when one questions the key assertion in a simile, it is only a step to more serious doubts. Does thought work *only* in silence; and virtue *only* in secrecy?

Not long afterwards I caught Tammas again, this time in his *French Revolution.*

"Time was," he says sonorously, "when men could (so to speak) of a given man, by nourishing and decorating him with fit appliances, to the due pitch, make themselves a king, almost as the Bees do, and what was still more to the purpose, loyally obey him when made."

It may seem a ridiculous waste of good honest indignation to pick flaws with literary similes, but I was at the moment in a mood to fly to the defense of my friends. If ever there was a non-monarchial society in this world, the bees have it—for better or worse. They make no king, they obey no king. They have indeed developed a wonderful mother-bee with a small brain, smaller than that of the worker-bee, and an immense capacity for laying eggs. This mother-bee has long been called a queen, but far from being obeyed, she is the willing and well-protected servant of her large family of communistic children, most of whom are sexless.

I suppose it is right enough of the poet to build his metaphors upon current knowledge, but it may be dangerous to his acceptability in after years. All along from the beginning the poets as well as the philosophers, watching from a distance the wonder of the hive society, have used the honeybee, or their mistaken knowledge of the honeybee, for complicated analogies, usually to point a moral or adorn a tale.

Plato compares the unemployed pauper class to the "walking drones in a hive." "Of these walking drones God has made some without stings and others with dreadful stings." (Which God, of course, did not do.) "Of the stingless class are those who in old age end as paupers; of the stingers come all the criminal class, as they are termed." All of which is as full of errors of fact as it could well be.

I confess humbly that in the earlier days I found a certain prideful pleasure in discovering such fusty references, but after I had lived with the bees summer and winter for many years, I began to be more cautious.

I remember once hooting, at least figuratively, at a poet who told in beautiful rhythms of *honeybees* working on *red* clover. He needed another foot in one of his lines and knew nothing either of bees or of clover. But one year, during a season of dry weather, I, myself, found honeybees working on red clover. It was the first time I had ever seen it and it was accounted for, I suppose, by the fact that the blossoms, having too little moisture, grew so small that the honeybee's tongue was long enough to reach the nectar. But this was certainly too rare an exception to excuse a poet with a true eye. Usually one sees only bumblebees in a red clover field.

One day I found this quotation in the Book of Proverbs:

"Hast thou found honey? Eat so much as is sufficient for thee, lest thou be filled therewith, and vomit it."

This led me to look up many other references to the honeybee. In the Bible I found ten or a dozen, and there may be others. I found some forty or fifty in Shakespeare's plays, I found that there were many in Aristotle, Plato, Virgil, Pliny, Leonardo da Vinci, and in most of the ancient writers. So many good and great men all down through the years have been interested in the honeybee and its doings.

"Can there be a more formal or better-ordered policy," asks Montaigne, "divided into so several charges and officers more constantly or better maintained than that of the bees?"

Afterwards I was interested to find a contradictory view, written by the "gloomy dean," Inge of England (this in the *British Quarterly Review*), who probably knew as little by contact with bees as Montaigne:

"The beehive is an appalling object lesson in state socialism carried to its logical consequences."

A whimsical incident in a letter written by Gilbert White is beautifully unadorned, as one would expect:

We had in this village more than twenty years ago an idiot boy, whom I well remember, who, from a child, showed a strong propensity to bees; they were his food, his amusement, his sole object. And as people of this caste have seldom more than one point in view, so this lad exerted all his faculties on this one pursuit. In the winter he dozed away his time . . . but in the summer he was all alert. . . . Honeybees, bumblebees, and wasps were his prey wherever he found them; he had no apprehensions from their stings, but would seize them *nudis manibus,* and at once disarm them of their weapons, and suck their bodies for the sake of their honeybags. . . . He was . . . very injurious to men that kept bees; for he would slide into their bee gardens . . . rap with his fingers on the hives, and so take the bees as they came out. . . . As he ran about he used to make a humming noise with his lips resembling the buzzing of bees. . . . He died, as I understand, before he arrived at manhood.

It is a wonder to me that after all these casual references in the books I was reading, I should have waited so long for the Great Particular Discovery which was to open for me a new world of interest and enthusiasm. It came about most unexpectedly—looking over a churchyard wall in England.

I was out for one of the many tramps I have made in that beautiful country. I had on my oldest, floppiest hat and my hobnail shoes, and I carried a small rucksack on my shoulder, which contained a sandwich or so, a few small books, a light raincoat, and some other trampers' necessities. I had decided to visit a few beekeepers on the way, if by chance I found any—as I had often done in my tramps in New England. I had the name of a beekeeper of whom I knew and had thought of visiting, but as on innumerable other occasions, I found so many interesting things to see and hear and think about, and I stopped so often by the way, that I never reached my correspondent's home. I did not realize it at the time, but Fate and Destiny had me by the hand.

When I came to a little old stone church by the roadside, with ivy thick upon the wall, I fell completely in love with it. I turned in at the gate and walked about the ancient churchyard, where there was actually the kind of yew tree which I thought grew only in Gray's poem. There were many mossy old stones, with curious and nearly indecipherable inscriptions, there were swallows in the eaves, and a bramble of rosebushes—all as it should be. And such tranquillity!

While I was wandering about, enjoying the sweet summer air and the scent of flowers, I was suddenly conscious of an intimately familiar sound—the humming of contented bees. When I looked up, I could see them in swift flight up and down, back and forth, over the wall behind the church. I needed no one to tell me that they came from a numerous stand of beehives.

The wall was a high one and covered with ivy, but I stepped up on a broken tombstone and looked over. There in the midst of one of the most delightful little gardens that ever I saw in my life was a spare, angular man, his head partly wrapped up in a colored veil, working with his bees. He did not see or hear me. I felt guilty at such an unwarranted intrusion—especially upon the privacy of an Englishman—but it made such a perfect picture of the contented beemaster, all so neat and happy, that I lingered. The house near by was as alluring as the garden, its ivy-covered walls, its ancient tile roof, and a bit of a porch where there was a table for tea, and comfortable chairs all about. Like so many of the best things an Englishman has, including his thoughts, it was concealed from the casual observer behind secure walls. One does not get easily to an Englishman or his garden!

My conscience having now begun to trouble me seriously, I decided to step down. I must have made some noise, or a quick movement, for my beemaster suddenly looked up at me. Instantly he twitched the colored veil from his head and with incredible dexterity seized a round, flat, black hat and clapped it on his bald head. It was indescribably comical. I could see at once that he was the much embarrassed vicar of the church.

There we were looking with paralyzed astonishment at each other, I balancing on top of my tombstone, and he in his garden with a look on his mild face of utter opprobrium, if not alarm. I knew I should have to act promptly or be forever cast into outer darkness; and I was suddenly aware that I wanted, at that moment, more than anything else in the world, to talk with that Englishman about his bees. I was hungry and thirsty for bee talk!

I changed feet on the precarious tombstone and tried desperately to think of just the right thing to say. Mere apologies would never mollify that Englishman, however mild he might look, however Christian he might feel. I knew I was breaking the eleventh commandment.

"I see," I began lamely, "that you are having the same trouble with queen cells that I have been having these many years."

He glanced swiftly at the open hive near him; but he made no response.

"Do you cut them out entirely, or just kill the larvae?"

Still no response.

"In America, where I live," I said, "most of us cut them out."

A look of relief and comprehension spread slowly over his telltale face. I was as sure of what was going on in his mind as though he spoke aloud:

"Oh! One of those crazy Americans!"

For who else in the world would ever have dreamed of climbing up on a tombstone and looking over his churchyard wall?

"I have never before in my life," I said, "seen a straw skep. I did not think there could be a single one left, even in England. I am very much interested."

He glanced quickly around at the old straw hive in the corner of the garden.

"Oh well," he said, "now, you know, I keep a skep— I mean there are not many skeps——"

He was in complete confusion. He did not know what to do with the American who had disturbed the peace of his garden.

"I say," he said, "don't stand up there. What are you standing on?"

"Why," I remarked, trying to maintain my balance, "on one of your tombstones."

He looked utterly horrified.

"I say, now, get down, get down. You'll fall."

I disappeared.

"I say there," he raised his voice, "are you safe?"

"I'm as safe as I would be if I were under the tombstone," I called back.

I could not help laughing—being now where he could not see me.

"I say!" came his agitated voice. "Are you there?"

"I'm here," I responded. I was greatly enjoying myself.

"Come around to the gate. Yes, by all means, come around to the gate."

He must have had still another shock when he saw me—in my dusty old clothes, with my bag on my back, but this time he was prepared and welcomed me—although somewhat gingerly.

We went at once into his garden and were soon deep in the fascinating discussion of the art of beekeeping. We compared English and American practices; and I was initiated into the mysteries of the straw skep, which I found he kept merely as an exhibit of ancient methods. Bees had been flying in that "close," he told me, for two hundred years, probably much longer.

So many beekeepers I have known have a turn for philosophy, and many, a quaint humor: both born of being much alone at their work, with the opportunity of observing the daily life of a wonderful and well-ordered society. For centuries, beekeeping has been a favorite avocation of English churchmen, and some of the best beemen in America—Langstroth, for example, who invented the modern beehive—have carried the wisdom they garnered as beemasters into their pulpits. Most beekeepers I have known also are keen observers and lovers of nature, at least to the extent of knowing the times and seasons of the flowers and the habits of bees and other insects—although few make the next long step, to being really scientific students.

I found my new acquaintance full of the lore and the lessons of the beefolk—and, if truth is told, several decades (at least) behind the latest knowledge of bee experimentation and the modern practices of the best beekeepers. He listened politely but without much interest in some of the new things I ventured to tell him, but how he did blossom out—once he had broken through his English aloofness—when he began telling me about the Ancient Beemasters (he spoke in capitals) he had known. How he did love old things, old tranquil places, ivied walls, and flowery corners—and the pleasant, deep humming of his busy hives. I began to like him more and more.

"Have you ever experimented with mead?" he asked me.

We had now adjourned to the porch for a cup of tea. He insisted that I stop for it.

"I've heard of mead these many years, but I never yet saw any."

"It was one of the great arts of the ancients," he said eagerly, "probably one of the earliest and most important uses of honey. The gods on Olympus drank it, and the singers of the Norse Sagas. And every old monk in England knew how to make it—and, I'm afraid, used entirely too much of it."

With that he ran into the house and brought out a bottle and two small wine glasses.

"I've been experimenting with it myself. The old books are full of recipes."

With what tender delight he filled my glass, and a much smaller one for himself. When he held it up to the light, I followed his example. It was of a rich, golden color.

"Did you ever see anything more beautiful?"

"Never," I said. "Never."

"And the bouquet!"—he held the glass to his nose, drawing in a full breath. I held mine to my nose.

"A breath from the vales of Hymettus," I said.

He looked at me gratefully.

"Yes, yes, a breath from the vales of Hymettus."

Now, I know very little about wine, but I noted that the first sips of the mead were like living fire; and a little later I was prepared to believe all the old stories I had heard about "the mighty drinkers of the North" and all the escapades of Jove and his gods and goddesses on Olympus.

When I inquired of my friend how he made his mead, he went into the house again and brought out a curious old leather-bound book. It looked to be two or three hundred years old, and indeed, I found these words on the title page: "Printed for Tho. Dring at ye corner of Chancery lane in Fleetftreet. 1681." It was called:

SYFTEMA AGRICULTURAE;
The Mystery of
HUSBANDRY
Discovered.

Treating of the feveral New and moft Advantagious Ways
OF
Tilling, Planting, Sowing, Manuring, Ordering, Improving
Of all forts of

| Gardens | | Meadows | | Corn-lands, |
| Orchards, | | Pastures | | Woods & Coppices. |

As alfo of
Fruits, Corn, Grain, Pulse, New-Hays, Cattle,
Fowl, Beasts, Bees, Silk-Worms, Fish, etc.

The whole WORK being of great Ufe and Advantage to all that delight in that moft NOBLE PRACTICE.

My friend showed me the curious old recipes on page 198 for making mead, with which he had experimented:

Take of *Honey* Clarified twenty pound, and of clear Water thirty two Gallons; mingle them well together, and boil that Liquor half away, and take off the Scum very clean, etc. and if you will have it of an *Aromatick* tafte, you may add this proportion of Ingredients: viz.

Flowers of *Elder, Rofemary,* and *Marjerom,* of each an handful; of *Cinamon* two Ounces, of *Cloves* fix Ounces, of *Ginger, Pepper,* and *Cardamon,* each two fcruples: Thefe will give it a pleafant tafte.

[47]

After hearing of all that was in that mead, including the ginger and pepper, I did not wonder at its potency.

But what interested me most was not the mead, nor my friend's prolix description of his making of it, but the old book itself. I took it in my hands and turned it over. I liked the feel of it: I read here and there a line or so, the quaint old English and the innumerable quotations from Virgil. All of it delighted me greatly. I think I fell in love with it on sight.

"Here," said I to my friend, the vicar, "is some information about bees that you and I do not know."

I read him aloud the sober description of how bee-keepers were to get their first colonies of bees:

Build a Houfe ten Cubits high, and ten broad, every fide equal to the other; let there be one door, four windows, on each fide one; bring an Ox into it 30 Months old, Flefhy and Fat, fet young fellows to kill him with Clubs, and break the Bones in pieces, but let them be fure they make him not bleed; nor ftrike too hard at firft; Let his Eyes, Ears, Noftrils, Mouth, and other paffages for evacuation be prefently ftopp'd with clean fine Linnen dipp'd in Pitch; lay him on his Back over a great quantity of Thyme, and let the Doors and Windows be Ftopp'd with Clay, that the Houfe be not perfpirable with Wind or Air. Three weeks after open the Windows on every fide, but that whereon the Wind blows; when it is fufficiently Air'd, clofe it up as before. Eleven days after when you open it, you fhall find it full of *Bees* in clufters, and nothing left of the Ox but Horns, Bones and Hair: The Kings (they fay) are bred of the Brains, the others of the Flefh.

The author, who signs himself "J. W., Gent." (his real name was John Worlidge), asserts that this method was used by "our Modern and Great Husbandman, old Mr. *Carew* of *Cornwal.*"

My friend and I laughed most heartily.

"They really believed it," he said.

Afterwards I was to learn that it was one of the oldest stories in the world. Samson, in the Bible, makes a riddle of it to confound his enemies:

"Out of the eater came forth meat, and out of the strong came forth sweetness."

It is in the ancient Greek literature, and both Virgil and Pliny tell it for sober truth.

I was completely fascinated by that old book, and I said to myself, then and there:

"Sooner or later, I'm going to own a copy of this old book by J. W., Gent."

I did not realize it then, but this experience and the secret resolution I made at that moment were to open a new and wholly delightful world for me—the world of the honeybee as he has lived down the years in books. I have before me as I write a copy of that very volume by Worlidge, which I found later (at a pretty penny!) in a London bookshop. It was the beginning of my collection of ancient bee books which has given me through the years no end of amusement, and when all is said, much enlargement of understanding.

I left my friend, the vicar, whom I had come greatly

to enjoy, and with whom I had spent several hours, with regret, and headed northward. When I got to Edinburgh a few days later, the first thing I did was to visit an old bookshop I had heard about.

A Fellowship of Curiosity

IV

A Fellowship of Curiosity

WHAT AMUSING CHAFFERING I had that morning in the ancient bookshop in the city of Edinburgh! It was a curious old place that one entered by a shabby door. The windows were dusty, and the building itself, so long it had stood there, seemed near toppling over backward. I had been in many an old bookstore before this and bought many an old book that I did not need, nor really want. This was before I was converted and had accepted the true faith of the booklover—which consists in being obsessed by one bright particular subject which in moments of complete rationality he suspects is not of supreme importance in the world, but which, at the time, completely absorbs him.

I wanted old bee books—without at the time knowing much about them. Most of the things in life we want most we know very little about, else we might not want them so much. I found a crusty old dealer sitting in an old chair, at an old, old table with piles of old books—old, dusty books, books with the lichens of time well grown upon them—piled all around him on the floor and stacked in the high cases on the walls. He was a dour-looking Scotsman, and the faint welcome he gave me when I came in disappeared when I told him what I wanted.

A thousand bibliomaniacs will seek a first edition of Charles Lamb to one who will seek a first edition of Charles Butler, who wrote the best early English book (though not the first) on bees and beekeeping. I think my Scotsman, who at a later time showed me with loving care some of his early Leigh Hunts and Lambs and Coleridges, had never even heard of Charles Butler. There was a half-irritated look on his face when he gave me leave to go down into the musty catacombs beneath his shop and examine for myself his "farmers' manuals," as he called them.

This suited me exactly: it gave me a sense of exploration and unhurried discovery. And indeed, I had never before seen such a place: where books by the thousand seemed slumbering in their last resting place. Dust and cobwebs everywhere; books in every state of deterioration and despair.

I stood on a broken chair and went through shelf after shelf of the books: so much ancient authority now utterly worthless, so many pages passionately devoted to recommending error and teaching traditional ignorance. I came at last upon a few bee books, mostly paper-covered manuals that might bring a penny or so on a remainder table. But I also found a leather-bound book which attracted me first for having most interesting old bookplates representing two generations of the Verney family, both Lord Willoughby de Broke. It was in excellent condition and was illustrated by twelve beautiful copper plates which pleased me greatly. The book was called *The Natural History of Bees* and was published in 1744. I was to learn later that it was a translation of a famous French book on bees, by Bazin. I had no idea, then, of its rarity or its value, but I knew I wanted it.

As I turned over the yellowing pages, I discovered on a flyleaf at the back various penciled notations made in ancient script, with *f*'s for *s*'s, by some early reader. My imagination took fire at once. Were these notes made by one of the Lords Willoughby? Or more likely by some peaceful-faced old English gardener? I was momentarily so much interested that I considered tramping down to the seat of the Verney family—wherever it might be—for I knew there must be a story behind those old bookplates and the written notes at the back. I should have liked to talk with a lord or two about bees! I didn't do it; I almost wish now that I had.

I went upstairs, finally, with well-blackened hands and a dab of soot on my nose. I had the book in my hand. I handed it to my Scotsman with as nonchalant an air as I could command. He looked at me as appraisingly as he did at the book. I may say I had on my old tramping clothes.

"Three shillings," said he.

"I'll take it," said I promptly.

"You are an American?" he asked.

"Yes," said I.

He looked positively chapfallen. Why hadn't he asked more?

I found that book offered later in a London exchange at £1. It is the only time in my life that I had such an experience—and with a Scotsman at that. Usually the shoe has been on the other foot, and I have carried away a book for which I have paid much more than its money value—but have gained a treasure I would not have parted with for twice what I expended.

This interest in the lore of the honeybee, which now began to expand out of all proportion to my means of affording such a hobby, added greatly to my ardor as a beekeeper. I did not hurry it: I bought (or was given) a book or so at a time, and in the long evenings at Amherst, sitting by my open fire, I would occasionally go back to those early chronicles, delighting myself with the quaint English, tracing the growth of ancient traditions regarding the life of the bee, amusing myself with fiery controversies over statements of facts, most of which were untrue. I began to correspond with students and booklovers—to say nothing of old bookdealers—in America and in Britain. As soon as ever it was learned that I was affiliated with "this particular craziness," as one of my friends called it, I began to get all sorts of curious information regarding early writings on bees and bee culture. Two of my good friends, both pundits connected with the Library of Congress in Washington, sent me many references that enlarged my knowledge. It is singular how, when a man begins to delve into a subject of unusual, if limited, interest, with no motive of money profit attached to it, he finds himself being drawn into a delightful fellowship of curiosity. The news that there is a new convert seems to spread through the ether, and one finds little centers of enthusiasm where he least expects them. A total stranger sent me a bee book from Japan! It seems a wonderful thing to me, living here in quiet Amherst, keeping my bees, how I have become a member of a small but delightful group of people quite as crazy as I am. We have no president or secretary, we collect no dues, we publish no journal. We live the manner of life we like, we read what interests us—and there is no constitution or bylaws to disturb us.

Of all these experiences, I think I have enjoyed none more than the letters I have received from people who have read my books and who like the same things I do, and these not only from America but from England and even Australia, New Zealand, and many other

places. None are better than those from beekeepers.
Here is one I had the other day from England:

I have been meaning to write and thank you for the book
I have mentioned, for I too am a lover of the country, and
live in the depths of it as far as modern progress and inventions will allow me, and most of all I am a lover of bees
and have my own hives—sixteen of them—set in a small
orchard where I spend many happy hours watching, and
trying to help them, and, I am afraid, in the end, robbing
them, but still, always careful to leave enough so that they
shall never want.

Last Saturday I did a foolish thing when manipulating
my best hive—putting on the fifth super of shallow frames
—and I paid for it—I had over thirty stings on my legs. Well,
I must have upset them, for daily, since then, the hive has
sent out a few of its inmates to harass me as soon as I go
near. Today I got to the hive very quietly and stood just
behind it and I apologised for my clumsiness and told the
bees who I was. A couple of bees flew out, buzzed around
for a few seconds, and went away. I deliberately went to
that hive several times, but since then, I have not been
molested. Most people would laugh. You, I think, will not?

"What a pleasant thing it would be," I said to myself
when I read this letter, "if I could drop in on this beemaster on a fine morning when he is apologizing to his
bees."

I should understand perfectly his feeling, and I
thought of all the interesting talk we might have.

One experience I had, after I had been for several

years slowly gathering old books on bees, gave a tre-
mendous impetus to my interest. Being again in England, I went to call on the best-known beemaster and bee
authority in all the kingdom. I had had some previous
correspondence with him and had long wished to meet
him face to face.

His name was Thomas William Cowan, and he lived
in Bristol. He had been, at one time, president of the
British Beekeepers' Association, and had written a number of excellent manuals and guidebooks on beekeeping.
What interested me most of all that summer morning,
when I entered his home, were the book-lined walls of
his library. I believe he had, at that time, one of the
largest independent collections of books on bees and
beekeeping in the world. I have never heard of a larger
one. He must have had thousands of books and pam-
phlets and journals—including many in French, Dutch,
German, Latin, and so on.

Since we were both seasoned beekeepers, we began
by discussing our own practices, those commonly used
in America compared with those in England, drifting
from that to the best modern books on the subject. This
led immediately to the ancient beemasters—and in less
than no time at all Mr. Cowan had in his hand a most
beautiful copy of Herebachius' *Foure Bookes of Hvs-
bandry*. It was "New Englished and encreafed by Bar-
naby Googe, Esquire" and published in London in
1601. It had the original sheepskin parchment binding

with rawhide clasps. (I now have a copy of that precious book in my own small collection.)

I could tell by the way he handled it, and by the look in his eye, that he loved it. I knew just how he felt.

Well, we were off! I was a mere tyro, but I did know enough to ask innumerable questions. I can see him now, starting up, "Yes indeed I have it—in two editions, the first and the fourth," and running to his shelves to get the book I had mentioned. The rarest and most precious books he had he called "plums."

We were suddenly aroused, and I considerably embarrassed, by being summoned to luncheon. We had already been talking three hours, though it seemed scarcely twenty minutes. I knew he was a busy man, and I had firmly determined, when I arrived, to take only a little of his time.

"Oh, but you are stopping for luncheon with us," he said.

I protested in vain. Both Mrs. Cowan and Miss Cowan, gracious and interesting women, joined in urging me.

After luncheon, Mr. Cowan and I went back to the study. I said that I would stop only a few minutes longer.

"I wanted to ask you," I said, "if you have the first edition of John Gedde's book——"

We were off again, and before I knew it, there was

Mrs. Cowan in the doorway smilingly summoning us to tea

There are few social institutions more delightful in all the world, or more perfectly ordered, than the English tea. I wish I were gifted with the graciousness of the pen to do justice to the charm of it.

I am almost ashamed to confess it, but I remained also to dinner! And after dinner we repaired again to the study and talked steadily until ten o'clock. I left just in time to catch the last bus into the city.

We had talked straightaway for more than ten hours. I did not try, at the last, to apologize at all, for I think my host enjoyed it fully as much as I did. Two men with the same hobby! Two men who not only kept bees, but collected bee books!

It was some time after this interesting visit that I was able to get a copy of the earliest, and probably the most precious, English book on beekeeping. To this day I recall the thrill I had when the dealer took it from his fireproof vault, held it a moment in his hand, then passed it to me.

"This is the book I wrote you about," he said, "*Hyll on Bees*—the oldest on that subject in the English language."

I had known of it for a long time, but I had never hoped to see a copy. I held it tenderly in my hand.

It was a small volume, printed in black letter, in the year 1568. It was bound in old calf with a gilt orna-

mental border. There were bookworm holes through a
few of the pages, and the names of various owners down
through the centuries written in unsuspected places,
imperfections which possibly reduced its money value,
but added to my interest. I delighted in the frontispiece,
a woodcut portrait of the author, "Aetatis 28," with his
thin beard and Elizabethan cap and rolling collar. The
book was at once a treasure and a temptation; and I
fell!

I can give no better idea of the contents of the book
than by quoting the title page:

A PLEAFAUNT INFTRUCTION
Of the parfit orderinge of Bees,
with the marueilous nature,
propertie and gouernement of them:
and the myraculous ufes, bothe of
their honny and waxe (feruing diuerfly)
as well in inwarde as outward caufes:
gathered out of the befte writers.

To Whiche Is Annexed,

a profitable treatife, intituled Certaine
hufbandly coniectures of dearth and plentie
for euer, and other matiers alfo meete for
hufbandmen to knowe. etc.

Which Is Now Englifhed,

by Thomas Hyll
Londoner
1568

My interest was greatly sharpened by the possession and examination of this ancient book. I thought of a certain little boy playing in a garden at Stratford-on-Avon, no doubt watching the bees in a neighboring garden, when this book first appeared. Who can say that the young Shakespeare, with his eager mind and keen curiosity, never saw it, or never read it? Who can say that Lord Bacon, then also a lad, with "the first great scientific mind the world had known," never had a copy in his hand? Never looked skeptically from the book to the bees themselves?

It was, indeed, the time of the new birth in the British Isles—the English Renaissance—and it is significant that this book by Hyll was a part of the turning of the English mind to the riches of Greece and Rome—in short, a summing up of the ancient knowledge of bees and beekeeping. It is not a good book, but a significant one. Hyll himself was a type familiar all down through the centuries—a clever, superficial chap, a borrowing reader, a ready writer: in short, a sixteenth-century hack, with a knowledge of what the awakening British mind would read and pay for. He was at one time a devotee of astrology; he wrote a book on the *Interpretation of Dreams*, another on *The Whole Arte of Phisiognomy*, and a curious *Contemplation of Mysteries*.

In his introduction to his book on bees, Hyll sets forth with seeming frankness "the authours out of whiche this treatife is gathered." Among them are Aristotle, Theophrastus, Pliny, Cato, Columella, Varro, Galen, "and fundrie others, whofe names be here omitted." A later writer, Charles Butler, a better man than he, complains that for all his apparent ingenuousness, "T. H. of London," as Hyll sometimes signed himself, in reality translated "word for word into English, as well as he could, a work by Georgius Pictorius," "a learned Physician," and that he concealed the author's name and "adventured to publish in his own name." Even ancient plagiarism is finally confounded!

I had considerable difficulty in securing a copy of the far better and greater book published forty-one years later (1609) by Charles Butler. It is a highly significant and important contribution to the "advancement of learning," as Bacon called it. It represented, so far as this small corner of knowledge is concerned, the next great step in the Renaissance. Hyll had boasted of the authors he had copied: he had gathered and Englished the old knowledge, most of which was wildly inaccurate. Butler was of a different type of mind: he looked at life itself or tried to; he was a forerunner of the scientific spirit that was to transform the world. He calls the first edition of his book, indeed, a treatise "wherein the truth found out by experience and diligent observation discovereth the idle and fond concepts which many have written anent this subject."

This Charles Butler, for his time, was a thorough-going scholar. He had "read" at Oxford and had settled down to a poor vicarage near Basingstoke, where he served the people of his neighborhood, and kept bees and wrote books, for forty-eight years. I like to think of him there in his garden, a poor man in worldly goods, but rich in the delights of a lively mind, and inspired by a passion to know. Like so many of those curious Elizabethans, he was eager to improve, if not reform, the world. He wrote a book on *The Principles of Musick in Singing and Setting,* and a Latin treatise on rhetoric, and an English grammar. He was irritated, as some of us are to this day, by the "capriciousness of English orthography" and made the highly sensible proposal that "men should write altogether according to the sound now generally received." He became such an enthusiast that he translated his own book on the honeybee into his strange new spelling. I have a copy of it (printed at Oxford in 1634) which is extremely difficult to read. In the middle of it, the words all in his phonetic spelling, is a stave of musical notes arranged in triple time to represent the humming of bees at the great moment of their swarming. It is arranged with "Mean" and "Tenor" facing one way, and "Bassus" and "Contratenor" the other way, so that four singers, holding the book between them and facing one another, can all join at one time in humming like the bees. I have never anywhere else seen anything like it. What delight that ancient vicar must have taken in serving all his hobbies in one bold stroke—his love of his bees, his interest in music, and his passion to correct English spelling.

But these things, amusing and interesting as they are, do not represent the chief value of the book; for Butler, by "experience and diligent observation," could report a great scientific discovery. He announced that the monarch bee of the hive was not a king, as people had believed from the beginning of time, but a queen! There had been suggestions of this discovery in earlier years, but Butler announced it with a trumpet blast—in the very name of his book:

THE FEMININE MONARCHIE

or

THE HISTERIE OF BEES

SHOWING

Their admirable Nature, and Properties;
Their Generation and Colonies;
Their Government, Loyalty, Art, Industry;
Enemies, Wars, Magnanimity, etc.
Together
With the right Ordering of them from time to time:
and the sweet Profit arising thereof.

For the first time in history, probably, a writer, daring to write about bees, was really looking at bees. The earlier writers, all down through history, including even the great ones like Virgil, copied myths that were current among the people or repeated what they found in older books. Once upon a time I read every reference in Shakespeare's plays to the honeybee, to see what the greatest of his time had of the new knowledge as compared with the old. He could have read both the book by Hyll, which quotes all the old writers, and he could have seen Butler's book, which appeared in 1609, when the poet was in his forty-fifth year and busily writing *Cymbeline*. There are lighted passages which, it is clear, must have come straight out of his boyhood observations in the Stratford countryside. There is even evidence, unearthed by Professor Roland Lewis, that bees were actually kept in the garden of the Shakespeare house. It is in a letter by one Robert Temple, writing at a time when the home was occupied by the poet's daughter, Suzanna, directing an agent to plant certain "shutes of vine" "neare the Bees." There is a passage or so in the plays which no man in my opinion could have written who had not seen bees at work, many and many a time, with his own eyes—as I could well show, if this were the place. But Shakespeare also accepted and used the old beliefs and myths—just as Virgil did. Shakespeare's master bee was a king, and one of his characters speaks of the bee "leaving her comb in the dead carrion."

Butler had also a naïve shrewdness that enabled him to capitalize on his discovery. Most of his studies were undoubtedly made during the glorious reign of Elizabeth, who died in 1603. When his book was ready in 1609, how could he launch it more cleverly than with a dedication to Queen Anne? He did it beautifully, with a salute to her "Most Excellent Majesty" from "the most ancient and invincible Monarch of the Earth"— his own Queen Bee. He informs Her Majesty of England that *his* princess, in her "beauty, majesty, prudence, chastity, temperance, taciturnity and other Princely feminine graces . . . marveileth to see herself surpassed"—by the excellences of the Queen of England.

Pretty good for an unknown vicar of a poverty-stricken vicarage far from the lights of London! But it was upon such men as he, living their own free lives, princes in their own rights as thinkers, able to address the sovereign on his or her own terms, that the true glory of England was built.

But Butler, even though he based his findings upon "experience and diligent observation," could no more escape wholly from the deep-seated traditions and myths of his time, or the moral and social taboos, than the freer scientists of this day. He was sincerely religious, a vicar of the Church of England, and it was his duty to teach good morals and a sound faith; and since the honeybee had always been held up as an exemplar of all the virtues, Butler gives the old preachments a delightful new turn in prescribing the qualities that a true beemaster must possess:

But if thou wilt have the favor of thy Bees that they sting thee not, thou must avoid such things as offend them: thou must not be (1) unchaste or (2) uncleanly: for impurity

& sluttishness (themselves being most chaste and neat) they utterly abhor: thou must not come among them (3) smelling of sweat, or having a stinking breath, caused either through eating of Leeks, Onions, Garlic, and the like, or by any other means: the noisomeness whereof is corrected with a cup of Beer: thou must not be given to (4) surfeiting and drunkenness: thou must not come (5) puffing and blowing unto them, neither hastily stir among them, nor violently defend thyself when they seem to threaten thee; but softly moving thy hand before thy face, gently put them by: and lastly, thou must be no Stranger unto them.

In a word, thou must be chaste, cleanly, sweet, sober, quiet, and familiar: so will they love thee, and know thee from all others.

According to the good vicar's rules, only a saint could keep bees. Well, I've known, in my time, one or two beekeepers who could qualify—almost!

Being the religious man he was, he was also anxious not to weaken the faith of any true believer, even if he himself questioned some of the myths of the books and of tradition. His presentation of some of the old beliefs is as fine an example of the casuistic struggle of a good mind between the new science and the old medievalism as ever I came across.

It was to be argued that if there was a true government in the hive, and a queen (or a king) to control it, why not a priest and a chapel? This is the cautious way he tells the story:

I have read of a greater knowledge than all this. How there were bees so wise and skillful, as not only to descry a certain little God-amighty, though he came among them in the likeness of a Wafer-cake, but also to build him an artificial Chapel. If I should relate the story, all men, I know, would not believe it: notwithstanding, because every man may make some use of it, you shall have it.

"A certain simple woman having some stalls of Bees, which yielded not unto her her desired profit, but did consume and die of the Murrain; made her moan to another woman more simple than herself: who gave her counsel to get a consecrated Host, and put it among them. According to whose advice she went to the Priest to receive the Host; which when she had done, she kept it in her mouth, and being come home again, she took it out, and put it into one of her hives. Whereupon the Murrain ceased and the honey abounded. The woman therefore, lifting up the hive at the due time to take out the honey, saw there (most strange to be seen) a Chapel built by the Bees, with an altar in it, the walls adorned by marvelous skill of archi- tecture, with windows conveniently set in their places: also a door and a steeple with bells. And the Host being laid upon the altar, the Bees making a sweet noise, flew round about it."

The good Butler goes on to discourse about this miracle as ingeniously as any old scholastic—or else he is studiously and darkly ironic:

But whether this do more argue the supernatural knowl- edge and skill of the Bees, or the miraculous power of the Host, or the spiritual craftiness of him, whose coming is by the working of Satan with all power and signs and lying wonders, some scrupulous skeptics may make a question, and presuming to examine every particular circumstance over narrowly, will make objections against the truth of the story: which, by their leaves, in the behalf of my author, I must not spare to answer. First, it may be they will object that the Host being held so long in the woman's mouth, could not choose but melt and mar. Indeed, if it did remain, as it was, a Wafer-cake, this were likely enough: but being turned into flesh, the case is altered. If they shall say that because it was now honey harvest, at which time good stalls, such as this was, are full of wax and honey, and therefore, there could not be room enough for a Chapel with a steeple and bells in it, I answer that this is as weak and simple as the former. For seeing it is known that a blacksmith of London did make a lock and a key so little that a fly could draw it, why should not

> The little smith of Notingham,
> Which doeth the work that no man can,

frame a little Chapel in a little room? But then perhaps they will reply, if we grant you this, yet how could the Bees fly about the altar in that little Chapel, seeing they are scarce able to fly in so narrow a close room as the empty hive? As for that, it may be a mistaking of a word, haply the woman said they did but crawl. If they shall ask how the woman could see the altar with the Host standing in the chancel, and the bells hanging in the steeple, seeing the waxen walls were not transparent, they may easily think that the Bees would give their dame leave to look in at the windows. And if they shall say that those bells being made of such metal would give but a weak sound when they were rung to Matins, they must consider the parishioners dwelt not far off. And so I think these captious critics will hold themselves contented.

He goes on cannily, as a good vicar should:

I doubt not, but some incredulous people will doubt this story and therefore perhaps they will suspect the whole narration, supposing it rather to be an unadvised device of some idle Monk, which, if he had consulted with them that have skill among Bees, might have made his tale more probable. Alleging, moreover, that therefore there is no mention made of any particular person, time, or place, lest the circumstances should disprove the matter itself. All which objections I could as easily answer as the former, if I thought it needful.

It seems to me I could write half a substantial volume on these old bee books and then not begin to exhaust the interest and amusement I have had of them. So much remains to be told of the strange things to be found in them, of the charlatans who played upon the ignorance of the people, of the development of new kinds of hives, of the interest of one of England's worst kings, Charles II, in beekeeping, but this is not a treatise on the lore of the honeybee, but upon the pleasant occupations of my life in the country. The bees indeed stimulated my interest in the books, and the books sent me back to the bees to consider them newly, and often with wonder and amusement that such mighty clouds of tradition and myth should have arisen to obscure the even greater wonder of their reality. After more than a quarter century of beekeeping, I doubt whether, even though we take great credit to ourselves for being scientific observers, we have more than begun to exhaust the mystery of the hive.

So many wintry evenings through the years when the bees are safe in their winter quarters have I spent looking into these curious old books. A fine fire of apple logs on my hearth, and my books piled all around, some to read, some to write in, I think of the friends, both bees and books, they have made me; and I am still longing to buy books I cannot afford.

Onion Field

V

Onion Field

1. THE PLANTING

ONE OF THE GREAT rewards of living in the country is the opportunity as well as the privilege of getting thoroughly acquainted with one's neighbors. The richest rewards of life, after all, come of a man's intense awareness of his surroundings—that is, the sense of beauty, if he enjoys the natural scene, and the delight in new and deeper understandings, if his chief interest is in his human associations. How men and women live —*all* men and women—what they think about, how they work, and love, and suffer—surely there is nothing richer or more fascinating to watch and to enjoy than this. One may find adventure on any hillside, romance in any valley—if he possess the eye to see it and the understanding to write it down.

But watching alone, enjoying alone, one learns presently, is never enough. If one would really understand, he must also play his part. It is not enough to look at men working; one must himself work. It is not enough to pity suffering; one must share it. And how know love without loving?

From the beginning of my experience here in this valley, I had a kind of longing to get more deeply into the common life I saw and felt stirring all around me. I had my own orchard, my garden, my little fields, and my bees. They were not enough. I enjoyed them, I got vast help and comfort from the new interests they presented and the good common labor they necessitated. I even got, and this with some pride, a certain product that we could use, and that we thought better than any we could buy—such as fresh pulled sweet corn; tomatoes gathered only when they were fully ripe; tender new sprouts of asparagus; and the earliest honey, well flavored, as I loved to think, from the open meadow where the bee pastures are. All these things were still not enough. I wanted to find out, by actual experience, how my farm neighbors lived and worked—what *they* got out of life.

It was only after a number of years of preparation, watching the common farm practices of our valley, and becoming acquainted with some of the farmers themselves, that I dared to experiment with the principal crop of our neighborhood, which was, at that time, onions. In trying onion growing, I knew well that I should touch the very heart of the valley life.

I had sage warnings.

"Farming," remarked big Bill McGee, who was one of my friendly mentors, "is a gambling business. You put a lot in the ante and never know whether you are going to get it out."

At another time he warned me:

"You can get your dollars in all right enough, but it's the devil and all to get 'em out."

I staked out a plot of about three and one-half acres near the top of my field. It is as good onion soil as there is in the valley, a river silt with scarcely a stone in it, fairly level, and sloping gently westward. It had been used years before for both onion and tobacco growing, and I had had it in corn and potatoes for several seasons, so that it was in good tilth.

The time was just after the Great War—the first Great War—when all farm products were in great demand and farm prices were high. Even though help was difficult to hire, and fertilizers at the highest known prices, Steve, the Polish man with whom I had made the usual share-and-share bargain of our valley, was full of confidence.

"We raise um big crop," he said. "We make money."

I myself was to have small fields of corn and potatoes near at hand in which I planned to do as much of the labor as possible with my own hands. I remember that one of the first real tasks connected with the undertaking was the mixing of five tons of fertilizer on the barn floor—a dusty, odoriferous, back-breaking job. The bouquet was not improved by the twenty-four loads of manure which we had drawn up from Waid's cattle yard and spread on the land.

We began plowing on April 16, following closely with the wheel-harrow. We limed the corn plot at the rate of a ton to the acre; the onion field had been limed the year before. From this time onward I began to keep a careful daily record of our work, which will give the best possible report of the subsequent happenings:

APRIL 23. Although it rained, Steve kept doggedly at the hauling and sowing of the fertilizer. The atmosphere hereabouts is full of the ripe odor of old, dry fish. He insists that he must get it done: the onion sowing is already late.

"He's a worker," I said to McGee.

"He's workin' for himself," said McGee, the cynical. "If he was workin' for me, you bet he wouldn't do it."

"Maybe that's the way to keep men producing," I said, venturing on a generalization: "Find some way for each man to work for himself—or feel that he is working for himself."

"You bet," said McGee, "and the Poles know it better'n we do. They get a little piece of land anywhere and make their wives and children work it while they go out for wages."

The Poles do not buy the hill farms, the cheap land, but insist on getting the best soil—soil that may be cultivated intensively and produce large crops per acre. They don't seem to care whether there is a house on the land or not.

"We build um house," they say cheerfully.

And they do it: poor places at first—but habitable.

APRIL 24. Although it rained heavily last night, we had the team on the land early—with the tooth harrow twice over. A hard wind helped in the drying. It was a cold day. Late in the afternoon we began with the nig harrow for the final treatment, and the soil is now a beautiful, fine seedbed, better pulverized and more uniform than most hand-raked garden plots.

APRIL 26. Steve began planting his onions at seven o'clock this morning and planted steadily, except for about half an hour around 4:30 P.M., when he went home for dinner, until nearly eight this evening, when it was too dark to see. He ran off his first row four hundred and fifty feet long by setting up a stake at the end of the field and heading his machine for it. He used no line, but his row was reasonably straight. He planted nearly three acres in this one day, walking, as I figure it, about twenty miles in doing it.

He uses an Iron Age planter which scatters the seeds through a steel snout, covers them with a concave-grooved wheel, and, by a reversible side bar, marks the next row. He plants thirteen inches apart.

"He rain tomorrow," said Steve. "Me plant um fast."

And fast he did plant them. I think I never saw his like for work. He assaults his job, jumps at it, rends it—and comes out of it smiling triumphantly. He came dashing up the hill this afternoon for additional seed, and we had to hurry him three and a half pounds more.

Never was there a finer sight than our onion field as it looks now: as smooth as a man's hand. With the planting rows plain upon it, it looks like a woven tapestry with these the woof—varying from a rich dark brown in the low spots to an ash gray where it is dry. It is a work of art. It is well done. No scamp work anywhere.

Out in Wisconsin, in early days, we should have considered three and a half acres a small matter, but when intensively cultivated, it requires an immense amount of work and a considerable investment of money. Good farms in many parts of the country can be bought for less money per acre than it has taken us to fit, fertilize, and plant that onion field in this one spring. But it is the only genuine agriculture, in that it employs every inch of the land to its highest possible capacity. It is scientific. It is thorough.

Mrs. Steve was on the field for the first time this morning—picking up grass clots and a few scattered stones. The two children followed her around the field.

APRIL 27. Steve finished sowing onions. He was here at daylight, for it looked like rain. We used exactly twenty pounds of seed for three and a half acres: a little

too much I think. Steve has also rented six acres of tobacco land of McGee and is putting that in. He started
his seedbeds some time ago and will have to step lively
to keep both onion and tobacco land going—especially
after the weeds begin to come.

I had an interesting talk today with J——, a typical
New England American farmer who lives near Belcher-
town. He furnishes a complete contrast to the Poles
of our neighborhood. He has quite a large farm, mostly
in hay. He raises "a little of everything"—"just enough
to keep us going"—a few apples, a couple of pigs, a few
fowls, three cows, "milk and butter for ourselves." He
grows oats and corn enough for his cattle and horses,
taps a few maple trees in the spring for syrup, practically "lives off the place." The only crops he had to sell
last year were his hay, for which he got a good price,
and about twenty bushels of beans. He is a highly intelligent man and a good worker, but with no notion
at all of modern intensive agriculture. When he needs
extra money, he works out, teaming, by the day; or he
sells a part of his land at a price he considers very high,
to a Pole. He thus sold seventy-five acres of his land last
year, and "got more fer it than I thought the hull farm
was wuth." He doesn't like to see the Poles crowding
in—but couldn't resist the price this particular one
offered. "John isn't such a bad fellow," said he, "when
you come to know him—but he lives in a terrible dirty
house."

I asked him whether John was farming the land he bought.

"Yes," said he, "and he's raisin' onions on one corner of it. I never thought it would raise onions at all."

This is a history often repeated here in the neighborhood.

It seems to me that if only I can *see* and *feel* the life here in this valley, just the men I can see working from my hillside (say), I can come, nearly, to the understanding of American life—indeed, modern life. Life is here as much as it is anywhere: and art is here too—if the artist is.

APRIL 29. "Never mind," says Billy McGee, when anyone remarks that the spring is late, "it will even up by June fifteenth."

Seeds that sink in water are good—the old test—but Steve preferred to soak his in his pocket. Just before he was ready to plant, he pulled out a hard bunch of soiled woolen cloth—wet. He unrolled the cloth and showed me a hundred, more or less, of germinating seeds.

"He grow good," said Steve.

MAY 12. The onions are coming up everywhere through the field—small, pale green knees breaking the soil. Steve came over with his scuffle hoe, but the onions are not up enough to warrant cultivation.

MAY 14. Rain; rain. The ground soaked. Many onion growers are having to replant seed—the first planting having rotted in the ground. Ours are coming all right, even in the wet spots. Our new ditches are giving great service.

I have let Steve use the edges of the field for vegetables, and he is preparing the land by forking out the quack grass roots with great labor.

MAY 15. What is the use of *me*, the landowner, in this connection? I do little, so far as knowledge of onion growing is concerned, that Steve, the Pole, cannot do as well or better. I furnish the land, the capital, and some of the tools, but they will produce no onions—unless Steve plants the seed, cultivates, weeds, harvests. I take chances of money gain—or of loss. Steve is sure of *some* return; but if the crop is small, my half may not pay me back for the capital I have expended.

In the long run, possession of land must be based upon efficiency of use. As population in the world increases and large food production becomes more vital, the holding of land unused or inefficiently used by private owners will become more and more intolerable. At present, there is inefficiency at every turn, leakages everywhere.

2. THE CULTIVATING

MAY 17. Steve is giving first cultivation to the onions with a double-bladed cultivator that straddles the rows.

The onions are coming strong. He showed me a specimen of the wireworm, which is already at work: a hard, yellow, active worm about half an inch long. Its head was entirely encased in an onion seed which had already thrown out a sprout about three fourths of an inch long. The worm eats through the seed and consumes the sprout to the surface of the ground and then attacks another seed and sprout. It is the advance guard of the enemy. In some wet or sour fields it is highly destructive; but we have limed three years in succession, so that we are not fearful.

MAY 28. Steve and his wife were here early this morning weeding on hands and knees. Very hot. The two children, a girl of four and a boy of three—sturdy little rascals—played in the packed footpath that runs around the field. Steve's wife put up a hammock near the "kissing coop" for the children, but they preferred the dusty field edges. She was here all day, crawling and weeding. About six-thirty she changed her skirt, put on her hat, rolled up the hammock, and started home. But she met Steve coming down the lane—I happened to see—and they turned back to the hot field. Steve had been working all day, harrowing and fertilizing his tobacco land, and should, I suppose, be properly tired. But the weeds in the onions are growing! Down on his knees he went and began weeding. A moment later his wife was at his side. The children cried a little, for they were tired and hungry and wanted to go home, but soon whimpered down. I wondered what an American family I know of, which keeps a nurse for each of their weakling children and a second girl to help the nurses, would say to this way of "raising" children! These two little Poles are magnificent physical specimens, and the boy, when clean, is really beautiful. At eight-thirty when it was too dark to see, the family trailed homeward, Steve carrying the little boy in his arms. Can these people be beaten?

JUNE 4. Steve was here at five-thirty, cultivating; his wife came about seven to help. She works steadily until about seven in the evening, when Steve comes back, and the two work until it is too dark to see—eight-thirty or later. They both go barefoot, and she takes off her skirt and puts on a pair of trousers. They have not yet finished the first weeding of the field. Fine growing weather. . . .

JUNE 5. Steve spread five hundred pounds more of fertilizer on the part of the field already weeded. Much troubled with several patches of water grass—a pale green, shiny, grasslike plant—a kind of sedge—that grows from a hard red bulb. It infests the wet places. Rain came this morning.

JUNE 14. Steve began cultivating and weeding again on the north side of the field. It was hot. Steve thinks he will have to surrender on the two patches of water

[87]

grass. They have got the better of him: the roots go deep and strangle the onions. All we can do is to cultivate the entire spot and plant rye or buckwheat.

"Maggot, he eat 'em," said Steve and showed me several of the small onion tops that had wilted down, and in some cases had rotted. Upon examination one could usually find a small, hard, white grub about one fourth inch long which had begun on the bulb, below ground, and had eaten clear up to the green stem. Sometimes this wipes out large areas and sometimes it hardly more than thins the rows. It is bad on the adjoining farm; not bad yet on ours.

Today I cut out a newspaper cartoon that exactly expresses a widely prevalent public attitude toward the farmer in America. The caption calls it "The National Game of Food Production." It shows an immense stadium crowded with a comfortably seated audience and labeled "Food Consumers." In the center of the vast arena is a single lone farmer with his old straw hat and his galluses, making the dirt fly with a big hoe. The audience is cheering him—as represented by the remarks curling up out of their mouths:

"Atta boy."

"I certainly enjoy watching him!"

"Good work."

"He never fails us."

"What if he'd quit?"

JULY 5. Yesterday was the Fourth of July. Steve and his wife celebrated the holiday by weeding onions. But they never work on Sundays. Onions looking fine; wet weather has helped them.

"He come eat um, the thrips," said Steve, and found me a sample where, in the axis of the green stems, the minute insect feared by all onion growers had begun to work. The onions never looked better at this time of year, but the thrips are here, and no one can tell what will happen.

JULY 9. It was hot; fine growing weather. Toward evening, showers gathered over Mt. Tom, and Steve came for the nitrate of soda.

"He rain," said Steve. "We sow um nit' soda; make um grow fast."

So he took down the hard wet bags (125 pounds each) and began sowing at the rate of about 200 pounds to the acre. He used a pail, which he carried on his left arm, and sowed in wide, even crescents, skillfully, with his right hand—strong, rhythmic movements, full of power and grace. He walked straddling one row of the onions, his shoulders well back, erect, and his body swinging freely, tirelessly, at his labor.

Steve's wife, who is a Ruthenian, speaks English better than he and is a specimen of perfect physical health. She can crawl from dawn to dark in the field and scarcely be tired—she tells me. She can bear a child every two years, and never seems to notice it. It is amazing.

Our onions look fine: the whole field now is an even green—the peculiar slaty onion green so different from an oat field or a meadow. Ours looks better far than the adjoining fields; but there are here and there spots which have a slightly yellow tinge. I examined them carefully. The damage is caused by the root maggots, which bore in and destroy the bulbs, so that some of the leaves wither, giving the slight touch of death to these spots. Sowing nitrate is supposed to improve this condition, I presume by stimulating the growth of the unaffected plants. Steve is having hard work keeping up with the weeds: some large pig weeds, smart weed, and now purslane are in evidence. I thought earlier in the year, when I was paying for fertilizers and having the plowing, liming, and cultivating done, that the landowner got the little end of the horn, but when I see the labor needed to cultivate and weed, these broiling July days, I change my mind. Steve and his wife work no eight or ten hours a day: they work twelve or fourteen, even more. The thrips have as yet caused no serious trouble.

JULY 17. The part of the onion field on which Steve put "nit' soda" can clearly be distinguished by virtue of a darker and richer green. Onions making remarkable growth.

JULY 27. It is notable to me, as I get better acquainted with these Polish people, to see what they can do. They are a vigorous race, still so recently from the land and the disciplines of life on the land, that they are willing to work long hours at anything that it is necessary to do, with their hands or their heads. The other day we had a young Polish student with us to supper. He told me his whole story. He is now about twenty-seven years old, son of a Galician Polish peasant. Never went to school until he was ten years old. Wanted more schooling, but his father determined that he should remain on the farm. He went to work in a brick-yard to earn money. He suddenly formed an ambition to come to America. "I scarcely knew why." It required four hundred korona ($80.00). He earned part, and his father finally gave him part, and in 1910 he migrated to Northampton. Began work in a basket shop at $1.00 a day. Went to evening school: was taught by Smith College girls. Suddenly conceived the idea of going ahead and getting a real education. Sent for circulars of a Polish high school, which would not take him unless he paid down $200.00, which he did not have. Discouraged, he told his Smith College teacher. She said, "Why, in America you can always get a chance for an education—if you are willing to work."

She wrote for a catalogue of Springfield College. He went there, learned English, and took his preparatory course. Afterward he entered Amherst College, graduating *cum laude,* with highest honors in history. Secured a scholarship at Harvard and is going there this fall to work for his doctorate. Is on fire with his work. He made his own way through college, earned his board by washing dishes, and his room by caring for a furnace.

He was brought up strictly a Catholic, but during his sophomore year read Paine's *Age of Reason.* Wrote an article for the Springfield *Republican* criticizing the Polish priests for their opposition to education and the public school in America. He was boarding then with a Polish family—good people. The priest protested to his landlady about harboring a heretic, and she turned him out.

He thinks one of the greatest things in America is free opportunity. It is no disgrace in this country for an ambitious youth, eager for an education, to earn money by any kind of labor. In Poland this would be impossible. His chief criticism of American life is that its emphasis is too much upon action, speed, and too little upon thought. Students seem to lack intellectual curiosity. They seem not to be interested in the great problems of the country and of the world. The chief passion of the Poles who live here, he says, is for land of their own. They become Americanized in one particular immediately—that is, in ambition to "get ahead" —get ahead in the American sense of making money and acquiring property.

When I asked him whether he thought that the Poles would Americanize rapidly in other ways, he asked:

"What do you mean by Americanize? Some Americans seem to think America means doing as little work as possible for as much money as possible, chewing gum, and going to the movies every night."

He told of meeting a woman in Hadley not long ago while waiting for a car. She asked him if he were a Pole. He said, "Yes." At once she began a kind of tirade against the Poles for coming into Hadley and buying up all the good land. Said her ancestors had lived at Hadley for two hundred years and that she thought it a shame for the Poles to be crowding the Americans out.

If the Americans more or less "look down" upon the Poles, so do the Poles, curiously, upon the Americans. They are a very ancient, vigorous, resistant stock, with their own tough-twisted traditions.

Afterward this young man, whose name was Stephen P. Mizwa, became a teacher at Drake University in Iowa, one of the most typically American of our colleges, and afterward helped to organize and became Executive Director of the Kosciusko Foundation, which arranges for the exchange of scholars between America and Poland. He is the author of *Great Men and Women of Poland*.

JULY 30. I went yesterday to attend the meeting of the onion growers of the valley and came away a humbler and a wiser man. I see I have ventured upon a highly skilled profession—a profession serious enough to engage a man's best brains during his entire life. We had discussions of onion pests—especially thrips, maggots, and smut—and how to deal with each. Onion storage was considered exhaustively and statistically as well as the onion crop of the nation in relation to the industry of the Connecticut Valley. Texas and California onions and, to some extent, Ohio onions compete with us in our own field of the Boston market. It was rather stunning to know how much more could be done, compared with what is being done, even in a form of agriculture so intensive as that of onion growing here in the valley. I had a keen inspiration to go into it more deeply, learn all there was to know, and raise onions as they ought to be raised.

The one thing most needed here, as this discussion plainly showed, is team play, co-operative effort among the producers. At present the growers, especially the small growers, do not get the full value out of their product. They are the victims of unscrupulous traders, of a want of storage facilities, and of capital, and they are at the mercy of transportation companies. There are as yet no accepted standards of size, quality, variety. A few big growers who own their own storage houses, their own trucks, and their own "brand" can succeed, but with the small grower it is a gamble every year. I am as likely to lose this year as to win.

AUGUST 7. Steve has finished his final weeding: at least he thinks it final. He has gone over the whole field two and a half times. It is now a beautiful dark green, with scarcely a weed visible. He came over today and walked about through the field stepping high over the rows, smoked a little cigarette, and contemplated with triumph his handiwork. What a fight he and his wife have had! And they've won.

It is the time of year when the grower begins to dream of his profits—before he knows what the prices are to be! Steve predicts a crop of one thousand bushels to the acre, which seems to be somewhat high. He predicts one thousand bags on the plot and expects $3.00 a bag.

"Get $3.00 a bag, I make um $1,500."

AUGUST 28. I dug and sold the first of my potatoes at $2.25. I am taking off supers of honey from my hives. No onion harvest yet in the valley, though some fields are ready; ours not quite yet. We have a large crop, but it looks now as though prices would not be as high as Steve so confidently predicts. Our Duchess of Oldenburg apples are now ready to eat—fine!

SEPTEMBER 3. This is the forecast of our onion crop as it looks now to me, according to the best estimates:

600 bu. to acre, 3 acres (net)   1,800 bu.
Bags @ 100 lbs.   900
Of these, 800 bags first qual-
  ity, 100 bags picklers

The price now is from $2.00 to $2.50 a bag. Say we sell at the low price (it was $2.50 to $3.00 for low last year) of $2.00 per bag:

800 bags @ $2.00	$1,600.00
100 bags @ 1.00	100.00
	$1,700.00
Of this, Steve and I would each get . .	$850.00
My total expenditure about	500.00
Leaving profit for me	$350.00

SEPTEMBER 10. One of the great valley sports now indulged in by everybody is the speculation upon the results of the year: the amount of crop and the price for it. A sanguine man can feel prosperous now for the next few weeks and ride in the imaginary automobile which he will buy with his profits. This year the sanguine men seem really to have the weight of evidence upon their side. The onions are actually there! And the price so far is unusually promising. Steve and his wife are calculating grandly. He got his tobacco all in last week. He says he will have five tons. And he counts one thousand bags of onions on our three and a half acres. He thinks he will get a gross return from the summer work of himself and wife, including both onions and tobacco, of three or four thousand dollars. Not bad for a foreigner without land of his own and with few tools except his bare hands. Remarkable indeed! Perhaps too remarkable.

SEPTEMBER 21. I found Steve and his wife crawling in the field yesterday, very dirty, but vigorous-looking. They have begun the final clearing away of the weeds in preparation for harvesting the onions. There has been so much rain recently that weeds have grown unusually late, and though they have not injured the onions, they are pretty thick. Steve and his wife throw them into windrows for burning. It will take at least a week for this weeding, and then they will begin harvesting their crop. I never saw finer onions than those in the lower corner of our field.

Steve has quite a lively imagination. He and his wife, as they crawl there in the dirt, with the two children following them, evidently discuss their future eagerly.

"Get plenty money, can buy automobile," Steve said to me laughing.

This represents the height of glory, as glory is recognized in this valley in this year of our Lord.

"Where you keep him?" jeers his practical wife. "No house, no barn."

"Sell horse, buggy, harness, everything for $200— buy automobile," continues Steve. "No can feed horse."

"No can feed automobile," observes his wife.

How very like Americans are these Poles!

"Get house first, get piece land," argues the sensible woman.

And this is what they will undoubtedly do: they will begin buying out another Yankee!

"Next year get big crop—more money—buy automo-bile," says the wife.

They'll have it too—next year or the year after.

"Me work hard this summer," said Steve.

"You have, indeed," I said.

"Rest this winter—big rest."

"Oh, you rest!" exclaims the knowledgeable wife. "He rest, two, three week, then go work wages. I know!"

He can make five or six dollars a day wages during the winter and probably will do it too.

These are the meek who are inheriting the earth of old New England.

At the same time, and incidentally, he has grown around the edges of my field enough potatoes, cabbages, carrots, beans (to say nothing of lesser vegetables) to take care of his family during most of the winter. His living expenses, therefore, ought to be low. I don't know what his rent is on the little house he occupies, but it is small. (I have found out: ten dollars a month.)

SEPTEMBER 26. Steve and wife are still hard at the late weeds; they have not yet finished the field.

We had a shock this morning when we read in the Springfield *Republican*:

Onions are now selling in the lot for about $1.25 per one hundred pounds. At this low price those fortunate enough to have a yield of eight or nine hundred bushels per acre will come out about even, but those who have only an average crop will lose money, and the Polish men, women and children who have labored from sunrise to sunset all summer will be poorly paid for their work.

If this is true, down come all our air castles!

3. THE HARVESTING

OCTOBER 1. Steve has finished the late weeding, though lashing rains in the first two days have started new ones, especially that most irritating of all the tribe: chickweed. They had uprooted practically all the onions in the field and raked them into long brown windrows, and today they have begun the top clipping. They use a kind of miniature sheep sheers, double-bladed. It is a big job. Prices still sag. Steve said he heard that onions had sold as low as 90¢ a bag. Think of it: 45¢ a bushel! In Hadley a day or so ago, when a buyer appeared, the Polish onion growers pursued him wildly in the town road shouting, "Buy my onions, buy my onions!" What a comment on the state of our agriculture! The utter want of organization.

OCTOBER 2. What days of golden beauty are these. The air clear, bracing—like heady wine. I have been cutting and shocking field corn, picking apples that the wind blew down—McIntoshes, Wolf Rivers, and Jonathans especially—and today the last of the peaches.

OCTOBER 6. What a job it is to handle every onion and clip off the top—in 2,000 bushels! This is what Steve and his wife are doing now. The two kids play in the piles of weeds heaped between the onion rows. I was cutting and shocking corn in the field near them today and was newly amazed at the ferocity with which Steve works—never missing a moment. Even when I go over to talk with him, his busy hands speed on. Tonight, when it was too dark to see, they started the weed piles burning; I saw their shadowy figures coming and going about the fires, damping them down with new fuel so that they sent off vast, dim, mystical clouds of smoke, variously lighted, in the cool night air—until suddenly they flamed bright again. I heard the children shouting with excitement. . . .

Our onions are very fine indeed. Yesterday Steve's wife came smiling to our door, bringing an apronful for us—the first fruits of the bountiful year. She did it with a beautiful simplicity and courtesy—making us feel, not that it was a traditional duty that had come down to her through her peasant forebears, but that we were friends and co-workers, that we should be as proud as she and Steve were of the fine crop we had raised. What fine thing could we do for them that would be simpler or sincerer than this?

The hard facts of the situation continue to develop: the market price of our onions is dropping lower and lower. The small growers (us!) have no chance at all.

We have no way to store our crops; and because we must have our money promptly, we are at the mercy of the buyers. . . .

A neighbor Pole and his wife are in their field near ours clipping their onions; they bring all five children with them—the oldest not eight, the youngest a baby in a cab. They push the cab into the shade among the tall cornstalks on the edge of my field, and the older girl looks after the baby while the mother sits on the ground and clips onion tops. I noticed that she was wearing the highest-heeled shoes that can be bought. The first adoption of America, by the women, is the flowered hat and high-heeled shoes.

I have been associated with these Poles in various ways for a number of years, and I like them. I like the courage and cheerfulness with which they meet the many difficulties of coming to a foreign land; learning a new language; forced, at first, to work at the hardest and least productive labor and at the lowest pay—and still going on, going on.

It is difficult to generalize regarding them, for they are as various in their gifts and capacities as we are ourselves. It is astonishing how swiftly many of them, in spite of every sort of disability, are able, in a land of relative freedom and opportunity like ours, to rise to places of responsibility, competency, and even wealth. They are now, the best of them, beginning to appear in our higher schools and in our political campaigns.

Some of the ablest football players of our eastern colleges are these powerfully built young Poles.

OCTOBER 20. Steve was out last night again with his lantern until near ten o'clock, clipping onions. Though he and his wife have worked fiercely for over two weeks, the field is not yet half harvested. He is a little behind the valley. Some fields are already clear, some crops are sacked, and nearly all are clipped.

NOVEMBER 4. A remarkable fall. No killing frost yet. Steve is nearly through with the topping, and has sacked about 500 bags of the onions, but it seems impossible to get any more bags. I went down to North Hadley this morning to try to find some. The prices of onions are shamelessly low. A large crop everywhere, most of the storage houses filled, and no one seems to want any more. I found two buyers this week, but they went over the ground critically and complainingly (as customary), and one would make no offer at all; the other proposed 70¢ a bag for firsts. Thirty-five cents a bushel! And we have yet to sort and haul them. I can stand the loss, but it is terribly hard on Steve and his wife, who have slaved in the hot field all summer with their children tagging after them. They will not make even Polish wages. If it were not for his tobacco (which, however, is not doing so well as he expected) he would be in hard shape this winter.

NOVEMBER 6. Well, our onions are sold—at a great loss. I went over with Steve in the afternoon yesterday to Sunderland meadows and succeeded in buying 600 more burlap bags at 5¢ each (I paid only 3¢ for the 150 I got the other day), to use in field storage. It has been almost impossible to get enough bags. I brought them home in the car—loaded like a furniture truck. Steve and wife at once began filling them in long, yellow-brown rows down the field. It looks now as though we should have 1,100–1,200 bags. Just at dusk came a buyer from Hadley and said he had an order for twelve carloads at $1.00 a bag, delivered f.o.b. Amherst. He would furnish bags (grass bags) at 15¢, and he expected to make 10¢ a bag for himself. He would pay us 75¢ for No. 1 onions and 45¢ a bag for picklers. We got this last arrangement only with difficulty, because picklers at this time of year are worth very little. He said he would pay us this whether he shipped them (the picklers) or left them on the ground. With freight to Boston at 23¢ a bag, there is very little in handling them. I talked with Steve and his wife (Mrs. Steve is an essential person in the bargain), and they finally agreed. It is now so late in the year, and so many onions are still on the ground (as we saw yesterday down in the onion flats), and all local storage is so completely filled, that it seemed best to sell at once. If we tried to move them to cover, it would mean constant expense and more work. So we all came up to my study, Steve smelling rankly of the earth, and the glib buyer drew up the agreement, which Steve painfully signed with many outbursts like this: "Good onions: damn cheap." "This good land: grow big onions: no money."

Well, it is hard indeed for him—after such a season's work!

NOVEMBER 10. It was a fine, crisp morning, with a cool wind blowing from the north, and the sun bright on the brown-clad hills. Steve began screening and bagging at 7:00 A.M. He has a Pole to help him (at $5.00 a day)—the first help he has hired this year. They place the screen, which is a double-inclined, troughlike affair, with slots in the bottom, and slung from a stout frame on short chains, so that it can be rocked back and forth.

They bring up the bagged onions from near at hand, step up on a box, and empty them bag by bag into the top of the screen. Then they shake the screen vigorously by hand. A cloud of dust blows off, and also the loose outer covering of the onions (which thus leaves them smooth and fine), and as they shake, the small onions or picklers slip through the slots to the second screen (in which the slots are set very close: one-half inch), so that only the dirt and very small onions will go through. The onions from the upper screen shake down into a bag attached and ready for them, and the picklers into a basket at the end of the lower screen. It is hard, dusty work—lifting 100 pound bags all day long, but it is a sight to see the vigor with which they do it. Mrs. Steve takes care of the lower screen and the picklers. I drove the old horse down into the field with the scales, for as each bag is filled, it must be weighed. The new grass bags weigh less than one-half pound, but it is the custom to allow 101 pounds for each filled bag. Steve is so expert that he can often tell exactly whether or not he has got 100 pounds in a bag. From time to time, the screen apparatus and the scales are moved to a new central point, and the bags are brought up either by hand or by wheelbarrow. The two men screened and sacked about 250 bags yesterday: a carload. It was an ideal day for it: cool, bright, and dry. The bags have now to be ear-tied and sewed, for which I supplied binding twine (at 30¢ a ball).

NOVEMBER 11. At four-thirty this morning, before I was up and while it was still pitch dark, I saw a curious dim light on my ceiling that I could not account for. I got up and looked out on the field below. There I saw a bright lantern light—I think two lanterns. Someone was working at the onions. It was not Steve, but his wife. She had been at it since four o'clock, tying and sewing the bags. She had about 150 done before the men came at seven-thirty and the screening began again. These bags are now ready for shipment.

Steve came with the two children soon after seven:

the little boy in his rabbit-skin cap and heavy coat. The first thing he did was to gather sticks from the field below and build a fire, for the morning was sharp with cold. All the roofs were white, and the grass; and the air has an icy feel. It is the first hard frost we have had this year, though not enough to injure the onions.

It came off bright, still, sunny, cool: one of those perfect, precious fall days, with the nipped yellow leaves of the maples eddying straight down, making heaps of gold at every roadside.

Whenever I go down, Steve and his wife have a smile for me. I haven't heard a grumbling word this season from either—though they are going to be greatly disappointed in the returns from the crop. There is a kind of robust health, buoyancy, fearlessness about both. They do not know what sickness is.

November 12. Light snow (the first) falling on the sacked onions in the field. Steve was over again at four or five o'clock this morning, sewing the bags. Two cars came on the afternoon freight. I made arrangements to have two teams to haul them. The owner wants the outrageous price of $9.00 a day each. The cars should have been here three or four days ago—but there is delay everywhere on the railroads.

November 13. More trouble! The north wind, which was heavy and cold last night, died down and we had a severe frost. The thermometer stood at 20 degrees this morning. I went down with Steve into the field. The grass was stiff and went black under our feet as we stepped; even the ground was dry white and hard. The onions in the top and sides of the bags were hard. Onions will stand a good deal of frost, but it would not do to ship them in this state. Steve had begun screening but I stopped him and countermanded the teams. The buyer called on the phone and gave the same advice. We will delay loading until Monday and let the frost get out of them—if it will!

"More freeze tonight, maybe," said Steve disconsolately.

"Maybe," I said, "but we can't help it."

It is hard on Steve and his wife. We may yet have to accept a reduction for the freezing. If we shipped in the present condition, they would arrive in Boston wet and soft and would bring next to nothing.

I can see now many things we could have done—if I had been a "big grower" with storage facilities or connections in Boston, or if I had been a merchant or speculator. Is it any wonder that farming is poor? The emphasis is not upon the grower's ability to produce a fine and large crop, but upon his gifts as a salesman, or as a storage speculator. *The emphasis must somehow be returned to farming.* There is little encouragement for men to continue on the land; better go off to the city or work for wages. I am exactly in the position of hundreds of the "little fellows," the Polish farmers and the small producers, here in the valley. Some of our neighbors (like the Polish farmer in the next field) have not even been able to sell their onions as yet.

I got a whiff of coffee odor as I lifted some of the new bags today. Most of them are from Colombia, in South America, and bear the words:

PRODUCIDO
EN
COLOMBIA
63½K.

Bags are also from Venezuela and Bolivia.

I wonder what the men who filled them first, with coffee from their tropic fields, would say to a fine frosty morning like this, with men in overcoats filling the sacks.

NOVEMBER 14. Steve hitched up his old horse yesterday and drove down toward Sunderland to see his Polish friends and talk over the freeze with them. Many were caught. He came back shivering. He is despondent—thinks we'll get only half price for the onions.

"See here, Steve," I said, "don't get worried. The onions have thawed quite a bit today."

"Him freeze tonight."

"I think it will," I said, "but not so much as last night. Now let's get together and cover the onions up."

With something actual to do, he began immediately

to cheer up. I went down myself to help. We moved the bags close together and covered them with burlap, bags, cornstalks, etc. It was quite a job, and we worked until it was too dark to see.

It is pretty hard on Steve after such a season's work— big crop, low prices, and now a freeze.

Today is much milder and sunny. If we get favorable weather today and not too much frost tonight, we may yet come out all right. Upon first thawing, the onions exude a few drops of water. If this dries up quickly, no harm is done.

NOVEMBER 15. Began loading with two teams this morning. Steve is screening. We found we had large cars and are putting in 300 bags to the car, two high. A third team came in the afternoon and we moved in all 27.6 tons of onions from the field during the day. Not bad. In the morning the ground was frozen so hard that heavy teams and loads did not break through the crust in the field—one slight advantage! We had to double teams up the hill. In the evening came the buyer, breezily, and left me a check for $225.00 for the first carload. It ought to have been at least $450.00.

The onions in the next field, owned by our poor Polish neighbor, are still standing in bags, neither screened nor sold. How is he going to feed his children this winter? There are going to be large losses everywhere. I am glad we sold when we did, even though the price was low. We are out of it and don't stand to take any more loss.

The Poles speak of the different attitude of the "buy-men" this year over last. This year they are critical, complaining, they beat down prices, and they have to be called for on the telephone. Last year, the producer was the upper man, and the buyers were begging for the onions at $2.75 to $3.50 a bag.

NOVEMBER 17. Another twist in the weather further hampers us. Before we were through hauling or screening last night, it began to snow. In the night it was rain, and it is sleet this morning. We were able, though with difficulty, to haul the final No. 1's this afternoon, 264 bags, though some bags were wet. The picklers were left on the ground.

I sold my onions this year for 75¢ a bag while consumers at Boston are paying at the rate of $2.00 to $4.00 a bag in small quantities, and a very much larger price in little retail stores. "High tariffs," which some stupid people are advocating, will merely make prices higher for the American consumer, and hence reduce the demand for onions. And what can a high tariff do to keep Texas onions out of the Boston market? What we all want is more food at lower prices, at the same time giving the farmer a livable income. What is needed is co-operation in storage and in marketing.

I can now sum up the sad story of the year's onion

experience for me. It cost me somewhat more than it would the ordinary farmer, for I had to hire teams for most of the hauling at very high prices, though I did not, on the other hand, have to keep them and stand that expense. Otherwise, my figures would represent closely the experience of all the small landowners of the valley:

Fertilizer for 3½ acres	$209.89
Manure, and hauling same, and plowing in fall	96.00
Lime, and hauling same	3.42
Labor mixing fertilizer, etc., etc.	12.00
3 days plowing and harrowing	27.00
Bags (½ cost—some can be used next year)	17.25
Twine	3.40
Hauling to cars	42.75
	$411.71
Received for onions	324.00
Loss	$87.71

I have not charged against this year's crop the expense of a tile drain I put down through the land, because it is a permanent improvement. This $87.71 represents a net loss on *money actually paid out* in growing the crop and does not include any charge for *my own labor*, for *rent* on the land, or for *taxes*. The real loss is thus very much greater. This is my experience with the season's work. That of Steve and his wife in one way is slightly better; in one way far worse. He and his wife together received $324.00 (less about $20.00 paid out for labor and $20.00 for onion seed)—otherwise, approximately $280.00 for their entire season's work—work early and late of the hardest kind. They at least get the money clear, and besides have raised vegetables enough on my land to furnish a considerable part of their living for this fall and winter. But if it were not for his tobacco (which is not turning out as well as he expected) Steve, with his $280.00 net, and a wife and two children to support in these times of high cost of living, would come near to starving this winter. Is there any encouragement for him to stay on the land? Other Poles about are making $4.00–$5.00 a day *wages* and working only eight or eight and a half hours a day. Just now, December 18, coal is being sold to these very Poles by dealers here at $23.00 *a ton.* (At the same time that coal is costing me—at prices I consider robbery—$17.00 a ton.) Think how much, this winter, they can afford to keep warm! Think how much clothing for a man, woman, and two children can be had after deducting rent for a house, fuel, and food from such an income.

I think these things, bad as they are, must be understood. I think they must be considered if we are to build up a sound democracy, based upon the general welfare, in America. We have never yet appreciated in America, however much we boast of our politically democratic form of life, the deep importance of the economic relationships of human beings. With cheap land, an expanding industry, and for years a rapidly increasing population, we have never needed to. But a new reckoning is now close upon us.

At the close of our discouraging season of onion growing, Steve remarked with emphasis:

"Me no more grow onions."

I fully agreed with him. No more onions for me!

But the next spring, I had a strange and deep experience. One fine Sunday afternoon in late March I walked down across my bare fields. It was one of those still, mild, beguiling days, prophesying spring, that come long before the spring really appears. Warm sunshine, a lazy south wind blowing—the newly arrived robins flying, and the bees in their first joyous escape from their dark winter boxes.

As I walked down the land, I had a moving sense of the land coming alive under my very eyes. The earth was indeed brown and bare, but it gave off a faint, sweet, unforgettable odor—or was it merely an imaginary emanation?—of stirring life. I stood there looking across the fields—with such a feeling of sympathy, and of understanding, as I cannot describe. They wanted me, they longed for me, those acres. They had been waiting, hoping I would come.

How could I let them lie there barren and dead? What was to be done with the willing earth, so full of potent life, so eager to produce? Land, too, that was mine —that would thrive if I smiled on it. . . .

I had the belief, inexpressibly deep, that somehow, really for the first time, I knew what the land had meant to inarticulate men for thousands of years, the renewed life in the spring, the toil of the summer, the harvests of the autumn—and the fruitfulness and the joy, and the sadness and the loss. . . .

I stood there a long time. . . .

Presently, at the top of the field I saw a man moving. He came slowly down the hill, walking across the bare, brown acres.

"You grow um onions this year?" asked Steve. "Me help."

Well, I continued in spite of all the difficulties, to grow onions for a number of years, each season certain that I had learned the bright particular lesson for avoiding the mistakes of the former season—each fall more or less disillusioned. But out of it, every year, came a satisfaction, a deep sense of fulfillment, that I would not have missed. Two years I made a small profit; two or three years I came out about even. I have grown older not unhappily.

Living in a Troubled World

VI

Living in a Troubled World

ONE WARM AFTERNOON, ten or a dozen years ago, I saw a forlorn, down-at-the-heels human being coming along my hillside and pausing uncertainly in my orchard, where I was at work with my bees. I had on my veil and gloves. As he approached, I could see plainly that he was in trouble and unhappy, so I said to him, on the spur of the moment:

"There is plenty of time. Why worry?"

He seemed considerably taken aback, and it was a moment or so before he responded.

"Well, I *am* in trouble, and I *am* unhappy."

I will not here go into the story which he poured out to me as we sat there in the shade of an apple tree, watching the busy flight of the bees. It was familiar enough in its essentials—a man misplaced and unsuccessful, a man with a miserable civil war going on in the citadel of his life, so that he had lost all sense of se-

[117]

curity, or usefulness, let alone any joy. He had "lost his grip," as he himself expressed it, and in the process, as so often happens, he had alienated his family and most of his friends. Loneliness is one of the penalties of such tragedies.

He wanted, as a last resort, to try living in the country. He had read *Adventures in Contentment* and others of my books and thought, as he explained, that I could help him with suggestions. He evidently believed that if he could get a little farm and live on it, his troubles would instantly disappear.

Many years ago, when I first came here, I usually encouraged such experiments, in the hope that they might be as happy in their result as mine have been for me. Afterward, in response to many letters and not a few visitors, I became more cautious. I held back: I raised a hundred obstacles based upon my own experience. For I had learned that country life in itself will work no miracle; the healing must come from within the man, not from without. I had come to love all the processes of the earth too much to think with equanimity of those who venture into its mysteries without removing their shoes—and their coats! Nature is shy, reserved, reluctant, and those who go to her must be willing to give far more, at first anyway, than they get. And yet a life on the land will help—*if* undertaken with determination and sincerity *by a man who has in the beginning some love of the country—and* a fair degree of health, *and* a little money. It will often help greatly; it will sometimes lead to a complete regeneration.

I think I said some of these discouraging things to my visitor.

"It seems to have worked for you," he said.

I responded that I was only a part-time farmer.

"I am a man with a profession trying to learn how to live," I said.

But these explanations, even as I made them, seemed an unworthy commentary upon what my small plot of ground and my life in the country had done for me. I knew well—or thought I knew—that I could never have lived through the years of studious labor to which I was inexorably committed if it had not been for my garden and orchard, and my little fields, and my honeybees. All the professions, if one is to succeed in them, require much concentrated and exacting labor; few more than the profession of the writer. No one can know, who has not had the actual experience, what anxious and prolonged labor goes into a biography or a history—or for that matter into a truly written novel or play, to say nothing of poetry—not the writing alone, but the infinite and judicious care and thought required in studying the materials to be used, and, where necessary, the sober weighing of contradictory evidence. I have spent many days, written many letters, conversed with many men—who usually disagreed in their evidence—to establish beyond peradventure a fact or facts that were to occupy only a line or two in my book.

When such labor as this becomes unendurable, what relief, what joy in being able to step out into one's garden and orchard, work in one's fields, or better still, attend to the engrossing and delightful tasks of the apiary. It was enough even to get one foot into the soil! With time and practice, I learned how to dismiss the irritating problems of my daily labor instantly from my mind and to enter with complete relief and joy into the daily round of my various avocations. I found also that I could increase and prolong these interests by writing about them. It was a joy scarcely secondary to the experiences themselves. So it was that *Adventures in Contentment* came into being, even before I came to Amherst, and *The Friendly Road,* and *The Countryman's Year,* and all the others. I was sometimes confounded with the fact that most readers enjoyed these books far more than the solemn literary works upon which I worked for so many years. Sometimes I was even jealous of myself!

I have often wondered whether I could have written these books, in which I took such delight, if they had not represented the release, the freedom I felt, and the joy, in turning from the heavy daily labor from which I made my living. The highest joy, somehow, cannot be had by frontal attack—one cannot find happiness if he seeks it as an occupation—for it comes indirectly, the incidental reward of toil and duty and suffering.

I knew these things were true for me; I knew also from my own acquaintance in the country that they were true of many other hard-working people—not only professional and business men, but office and factory and railroad workers. What could I say, then, to my unhappy visitor there under the apple tree?

Well, I made out as bad a case as I could, and was somehow deeply delighted when he said obstinately,

"I'm going to try it anyhow."

He thanked me and walked away up the hill. I imagined that he stepped more firmly than he did when coming down, but this may have been due to a kind of sympathy—irritated sympathy!—he seemed to have awakened in me.

I should like to bring off this particular story with a wholly comfortable and happy ending. He has, in fact, had a pretty hard time of it—but to me the main thing is that he and his family are still on the land, that he has learned to work with his hands, that he takes pride in what he raises. He says he has "a greater sense of security" than ever before in his life.

"If worse comes to worse," he said, "I know my land will not go back on me. I know that we can at least raise enough with our own hands to live on. You don't know how much that means to us!"

Who knows what the future still has in store for

him? Who knows what his life will be like when he has been on his land as long as I have on mine?

My friend's experience is in no way unusual. In this part of New England we have few really large farms, and many of the small holdings, especially around the small manufacturing cities, are occupied by genuine part-time farmers. I have known some of these men and their families for many years. In tramping up and down the valley, I have sometimes called on one or another of them. Some of them are factory workers who have relatively short hours of daily work with free Saturday afternoons—sometimes all day Saturday. Since all of them own their own cars—the low-priced automobile has been a truly revolutionary influence in American country life—they can get quickly from their working place to the little farm four or five or even ten miles out in the country. I know such men who started with practically nothing, built their houses and barns and chicken coops largely with their own hands, and soon began raising enough to provide most of their food. If the wife and children in the family are industrious and thrifty, they can have a cow or two, chickens and turkeys, and, best of all, if they have the turn for it, keep a few stands of honeybees. It is wonderful to me to see what some of these families have done—and how much they enjoy it. I know one such place, kept by a railroad fireman—who says he "works on the railroad so that he can live on a farm"—where the wife and children produce broilers as their cash crop. At another place the specialty is blackberries. I never saw a better "patch" anywhere than this one—cleanly cultivated, well staked, and well pruned. It is on a favorable hillside and produces abundantly and profitably every year. Another family I know—the husband is an architect whose work is in a city—raises the new cultivated blueberries, and this year has a flock of ducks. Another is a specialist in bantam fowls and has taken prizes in the best shows in America for Silver Sea Brights, Black Rose Combs, and Partridge Cochins. Still another, also a railroad man, who came to the land without any experience whatever, has now a most interesting place. He has built some of the buildings himself, working during the early mornings or late afternoons, or on Saturdays. He has a tractor, which he put together himself, using old machine parts that cost him little or nothing. He owns several fine Jersey cows, a large flock of White Wyandottes, a thrifty garden, and a newly planted orchard. Work? Of course he works, and his wife works, and his children work—and they are blessed accordingly.

I know of several men and their wives who are graduates of famous classical colleges who are living on farms, and doing well. Their reasons are as various as those in any calling. Some of them thoroughly enjoy it, and are not only successful in their work, but have become active and able leaders in their communities. Others are the type of restless experimenters who will probably be soon discouraged and pass on to something else.

Few of the part-time farmers I know, or know about, are at all self-analytical—any more than most other human beings. Why are they on the land? Why, "because I like it." One says, "I love being independent"; another, "It's the kids. There's no place like a farm to bring up children. They learn how to work and how to co-operate." Several will tell you that they "feel better in the country." "All of us are healthier since we came out here." Health is often the determining factor.

But the chief reason, as it seems to me, though it is not so often or so clearly expressed as some of the others I have mentioned, is the sense of security so many of these people have, or come to have. A machine-tool worker I was talking with recently expressed it exactly.

"We feel somehow safe here on this little place. If I lose my job, or there's a strike in the factory, or one of us has a long sickness, why we're here and can live for a long time without being scared. It's only a little place, but you'd be surprised to see how much we can raise on it. We have a cow and chickens; we can grow enough potatoes and vegetables to keep us most of the year round. We have a little field up there on the hillside with nearly enough summer pasture for the cow. And we're all husky, so that we never have to hire anything done."

I know, on the other hand, at least one such establishment where there is black discouragement—due

largely to human incompatibilities and human inefficiency, for there are people who will never be happy or
successful anywhere, in any occupation—but most of
these part-time farmers seem to me far more contented,
hopeful, even happy, than average human beings. I may
be wrong, but this is my ripe conclusion.

"Lord," says one of the men I know, "nobody knows
what a joy it is just to see things grow, to be producing
something really valuable, unless he has tried it himself."

I base my conclusions not alone on instances I myself know about, here in this valley, but I have had
overwhelming evidence from letters I have received over
a long period of time. In the years since I have lived
in the country, and have written of my own adventures
and enjoyment, I have heard from hundreds of people
in all parts of the country, and even from Canada and
England and Australia and elsewhere, giving me truth-
ful and spontaneous evidences of what life on the land
means to them.

Wherever I have gone in my life, whether in New
England or Florida or California—or England or France
—I have found the earth, lying there patient and beautiful according to its nature, waiting humbly to be known.
And in every place I have visited, here or abroad, there
are fortunate people who know it and love it—whose
lives have been enriched by it.

I think also, and often, of the good fortune I have had

to be living in a country where a man has some choice as to his way of life and the work he is best fitted to do. It is only in the free atmosphere of such a land, deeply beloved by me, that a man may truly act his own nature and make good the faculties of himself.

I know no better way to set forth the experiences of these fortunate ones than by reproducing a few of the many recent letters I have received.

Here is one from O. L. Sanford, Jr., an accountant for a pipe-line company in Missouri:

Until two years ago I lived in town on a busy street and near a trolley line. At work and at home—typewriters, adding machines, telephones, streetcars, motorcars, etc. I rushed from home to office and from office to home, and the more I rushed, the worse my disposition became.

Two years ago my father, who had retired to a two-acre place twelve miles into the country, died. To make a suitable home for my mother, we moved to the country—feeling like martyrs.

Since then, my ten-year-old son and I have raised a pig (and made love to her). We butchered her and cured the meat, and then had little enough heart to eat it. *We produced something.* Of course we gardened, raised vegetables, fruit, berries, and chickens—even a few cotton plants. I have eaten meals produced mostly by my own efforts.

If my time is of any value, then my crops are dear, but the cost and value of them cannot be told in mournful numbers.

I'm an accountant, and I work hard with figures and papers and phone calls, and when my day's work is done, I haven't produced a solitary thing—but out there the lettuce and beans and fruit and berries are thriving with my help and for my pleasure.

Then there's the "Little Guy." He now has responsibilities, he's learning to work with his hands, he's learning about reproduction of plants and animals bit by bit, and he loves it too. I pray that I can help to keep him at it.

I could go on reciting the pleasures and thrills of it all, but I won't, for you know them too. Some day, God willing, I'm going to own a farm of my own, with trees and creeks and hills and fences and all that goes with them. Then office machines and office hours, trolleycars and motorcars won't count.

A police captain, Charles D. Winslow, of Grand Rapids, Michigan, has written me many delightful letters about his experiences in the country.

On the twentieth of July 1938, with the consent and cooperation of my wife, I purchased a run-down 40 acres, 53 miles southeast of this city. It had a poor man's house, built in installments and by people of three generations in meager circumstances. A barn wall still stands, a monument to a still operated within its walls during Prohibition times. Some day I will build another barn there. A chicken coop was torn down to improve the scenery, and because, something like you, I am not overly fond of chickens.

We do not live on the farm, but on week ends we hie away farmward, returning late on Sunday evenings. Our two girls have slept many hundreds of miles returning from the farm after bedtime!

I have seven acres of marsh, with a marl deposit in excess of 9 feet deep extending under much of it. I have a large spring which feeds a 15-acre lake on the next forty back. I have tamaracks, elms, poplars, red osier dogweed and yellow dogwood, water cress, and muskrat runways. I have a few wild blackberries. We have planted pieplant (25 hills), 450 asparagus, 100 assorted grapes, 10 assorted fruit trees (we picked 114 quarts of strawberries this summer); we have red raspberries and will, through our own efforts, have over (I believe) 50 bushels of potatoes. I plowed the old lane in 1939, sowed sweet clover, and in 1940 planted 9½ rows of late potatoes, each row about 25 rods long. Talk about soil for potatoes! I believe that lane was in sod for over thirty years. Later it will again be in sod.

From our "farm" I have received my share of life's joy. My wife, village born and bred, is the perfect partner in the venture.

Each week end we are at the farm. We have a lovely garden. Sweet corn, string beans, 2 plantings of late potatoes, 114 tomato plants (starting to bloom), cucumbers, 400 feet of pea rows, lettuce, kohlrabi, salsify, beets, carrots, and all others except that I completely forgot the first planting of radishes (which do not agree with my digestion anyhow).

This morning I returned to the office after five whole days of real enjoyment, which consisted of really hard work, at Bellefontaine Farm.

I saw the sun rise every morning but one, and worked on my pipe line, a reversal of your ditch in *Adventures in Contentment.*

He goes on, with a zest that delights me and that I entirely understand, to tell of all the interesting, minute, common activities of his farm and garden.

What I needed was a change of work and scenery, and the hard work at the farm proves to me that one can refresh oneself merely by changing one's line of endeavor—provided, however, that the change is toward something one likes to do.

And I like to improve Bellefontaine Farm. Not for the monetary value it will gain from the improvements. More, I guess, because it is like a stray dog, or an old, bony horse which has been overworked and underfed by previous owners. Some kindness, some rest and humane treatment and, like an abused animal, soil will show improvement and, I think, gratitude for favors rendered. Already the farm shows, in places, the beneficial effects of being groomed, of being fed after starving for years. My two acres of alfalfa planted in 1940 are beautiful—on what was the poorest soil on the farm. My two acres seeded again in 1941, after killing out last winter, received the rain of two weeks ago and are a soft lovely green.

So many of the letters I have received from country lovers reveal a deep interest in new and interesting experiments—as in this from R. G. Kelley of Clarence, Iowa:

The joy and satisfaction you get from growing things and the land are practically the same as mine. The work sometimes pushes one a little faster than one likes to go, yet all in all, it is a most satisfactory mode of living. I look with dread upon the day when circumstances may force me to leave it.

One of my main hobbies is a study of the relative nutritional value of food from rich and poor land. Does anything in history disclose whether any nation's downfall can be traced to land mistreatment?

I have even strayed so far away from the orthodox chiseling of the present generation as to recommend that each farmer be required to put up suitable collateral guaranteeing proper land use. Ownership of land is a trust, and not a license to exploit or destroy.

We are starting to make our alfalfa hay, we have 55 acres. We had some badly needed rain lately. Crops are looking good.

We milk 14 cows, have 157 pigs, feeding 64 heifers and 100 steers, 623 acres in farm. You can readily see that we are kept reasonably busy.

Such letters as these—and they are only a few among many—are vastly satisfying and encouraging to me. There is something wholesomely normal, cheerful, healthy, about so many of these letters. I like to receive them, I like to read them, especially at a time like this when the whole world seems to be going mad—when hatred and greed and fear and force are abroad in the world, and no end seems anywhere in sight. I keep thinking that the rejuvenation, when it comes, will come out of the land and the people who live freely, laboriously, productively, joyfully, upon it. What an anchor to windward in a storm like this now raging across the world! All stored property—all stocks, bonds, all hived-up gold and silver, all paper wealth, may go off with the wind, but the land remains, and a man's faith in his own courage and strength.

I think often, these days, of a trip I made in the spring after the close of the Great War, in April 1919, through the devastated regions of northern France. I saw the ruined cities, broken walls and rubble, wrecked cathedrals, devastated public buildings, and miles and miles of once pleasant homes all laid waste. I saw Rheims and Noyon; I saw Soissons and Amiens. Most of the streets were still impassable; and everywhere, up and down, there was solitude, and ashes and dust.

I saw many little villages that had once been beautiful, razed to the ground, with scarcely a remaining evidence of human habitation. Everything gone; civilization destroyed. It was beyond words melancholy and depressing. It was past tears: an indescribable weight of hopelessness upon one's spirit. I thought of James Stephen's lament:

> *For all is gone—all comely quality,*
> *All gentleness and hospitality,*
> *All courtesy and merriment is gone;*
> *Nothing is whole that could be broke; no thing*
> *Remains to us of all that was our own.*[1]

From one such little village I remember tramping out into the open country. The great trees along the roadsides had all been shot down, but the ruin had been somewhat cleared away so that a man afoot and even a cart could pass by. Every farm was in utter ruin, every

[1]*Reincarnations*, Macmillan, 1918.

shed, every tree, even the soil itself, cultivated with loving care for a thousand years, had been torn up. Deep trenches, holes where bombs or shells had fallen, and all about, everywhere, rubbish and ruin. Presently I saw men working. There they were in the fields, slow, gray, patient men, filling up the holes and smoothing away the trenches. In one place, near a ruined home, two men and their women where digging with their own hands, for they had no cattle—turning the soil over, getting ready to put in a few seeds. They were living, I could see, in a miserable hovel built of rubble and brush and mud. Two or three half-wild children, ragged and unclean, looked out at me as I passed.

I stood there a long time looking at those men and that dismal scene. It came to me with indescribable power that here was new hope, here was the new life, here was *beauty*. Here were men back on the land, patiently digging, sowing, harvesting, as always there have been from the beginning of time. These men, I thought, will again save the world.

My Elm Tree

VII

My Elm Tree

ALL MY LIFE I have been a lover of trees, as my father was before me; and of all the trees that ever I knew, I have loved none better than my elm.

My elm is one of the noblest in this town. It stands upward toward the sky seventy feet or more, with a stout bole some sixteen feet in circumference to make strong its hold upon the earth. It has both strength and beauty. It spreads its lacy verdure, a graceful plume of green, wide-spaced upon the meadow; and from the swaying boughs, drooping downward, hang airy hammocks for the orioles. One season or two, piratical kingbirds have nested among the fastnesses of the upper branches; and squirrels that feed upon the acorns of near-by pin oaks have found secret hiding places to rear their young. Once I saw a great owl perched there, turning its head solemnly in the bright, unwelcome sunlight.

I made the acquaintance of my elm more than thirty years ago, when we first came to Amherst. It stands a short distance eastward from the line of the farmland we bought for our home, so that when the sun first rises out of the Pelham hills of a summer morning, the shadow reaches across my study windows. Summer and winter, spring and fall, all these many years, it has been our constant companion, sometimes a responsibility, far oftener an inspiration, always a thing of beauty. It seems as much a part of the landscape as Mount Norwottuck, with equal simplicity and dignity, and far more personality. It is like some noble old man to whom, with long life, has come tranquillity. We have only to look out and look up to learn again what serenity may mean in a troubled world.

The meadow on which the elm stood did not belong to us, but we had our harvests of beauty from it year after year as though it were our own. We were quite oblivious of line fences and title deeds. We took what we would by that right of eminent domain with which every man who loves nobility, and can see beauty, is endowed. How post a landscape against the possessive eye of the artist, the soul of the poet, or the heart of the true lover?

We learned one spring, to our utter dismay, that we might lose our elm. The land where it stood was controlled by a neighbor of ours, a blind old man, who had been retired for several years. He lived in a small white house on the hill above us—we could just see his roof. On pleasant days he sat on his porch in the sunshine or walked with his cane, touching the porch rail or feeling for the steps within the narrow range of his yard. As I passed by in the road I turned in sometimes to talk with him, since he lived in a lonely world. He was a rather barren old man, though not morose. He liked to talk about his early days—"when I was a real man"— and the crops he had raised, and the prices he got for them.

One day, quite casually, I mentioned the great elm at the foot of his meadow land, what a beautiful tree it was, and how much we had enjoyed it in all the years we had lived in Amherst. I saw for the first time a look of strong emotion in his face. Even his blind eyes seemed alive. He brought his cane suddenly and sharply down upon the porch boards and cried out,

"It shades my pasture; it shades my pasture."

I did not at first understand what he meant, or the reason for his vehemence, but it was soon clear to me. While he could no longer see the great tree, he well remembered that it shaded a large space in his fertile meadow. Good grassland kept down!

I began, somewhat unwisely, to argue with him, that the elm now had more value for its beauty than the land for its corn or its grass. I shall never forget the passion with which he replied.

"Who gets the beauty? I don't."

Poor blind old man!

Even when I suggested, knowing the value of such an argument among us who are New Englanders, that it might add positive money value to the land for some future purchaser, he responded,

" 'Tain't no place for a tree."

"As for value," he added, "there's enough wood in that tree, even if it *is* an elm, to run my stoves all o' three winters."

I soon learned how hopeless it was. My neighbor had been a good man, but he had come down, the hard years, out of an age when trees were enemies to be remorselessly destroyed, their very roots grubbed out and burned. The ideal of the early settler, inured to the struggle with the forest, was what he called "cleared land." He liked a bare house set in a bare field, the symbol of complete conquest. It was not until the late eighteen hundreds that the settlers began to think of planting trees or of beautifying their homes with anything except flowers. The early pictures of this town of Amherst, now so glorious for its trees, show it strangely barren.

We continued to be anxious about the fate of the elm. I think we loved it even more deeply than before, as we love beautiful things that we are fearful of losing. One year when the elm-leaf beetle, then a pest in our countryside, threatened to be serious, I surreptitiously sowed fertilizer on my neighbor's meadow, all about the rootings of the great tree, to encourage it in its struggle for life.

As the old man grew feebler, his animosity to the great elm in his meadow seemed to grow more virulent. Behind his blind eyes the tree evidently became an even more menacing symbol of past enmities. He imagined, I think, that it had grown and spread until it covered a large part of his meadow—gnawing away at the fertility of his soil. Once when I saw him, he seemed almost in a rage.

"Can't I do what I please with it? I ain't going to stand no such tree on my land."

Old, blind, feeble, it was the last symbol of his power.

A few days later I heard to my consternation that he had been bargaining with a woodsman to have it cut down. Presently I saw the woodsman himself there in the grassland, walking around the great tree, viewing it with a calculating eye.

I was now really alarmed. Within a year or two we had seen one other such noble tree that grew in the valley below us remorselessly cut out, and for no better reason. That afternoon, as though casually, I dropped in to see my neighbor. I found him sitting, tremulous, in utter darkness, there in the bright sunshine, a figure of infinite pathos. I knew that he had spoken for years of selling his meadow, and yet when I hinted vaguely that I might be willing to buy it, he sat instantly erect and raised his head as though listening intently.

"You want that elm tree," he said in a high-pitched voice.

I could see that there was nothing to be done. The very fact that I was siding with the tree seemed only to harden his purpose.

I had one further recourse. In our town there is a law, blessed to all lovers of nature, that no street tree can be cut, even by the order of the sovereign selectmen, if there are widespread objections from the citizens. The tree is formally posted by the tree warden, and, like a suspect, summoned to court. A meeting at the Town Hall is appointed, and a trial is held. Shall the tree be slaughtered in the name of progress, or shall progress, represented, say, by a new street or a new curbing, be required to go around, and leave beauty to bless the eyes of men? I had been a fascinated spectator of more than one of these public trials, finding myself always siding with the culprit. When the practical issue is not too powerful or the new road too important, we will side with beauty any time! More than one great tree in our elm-shaded streets is alive today because of the vote of free citizens.

I decided to demand a trial for my elm. I thought, as I hurried into the town, of the eloquent case I could make for it. I could and would argue the worth of beauty—even the practical worth of beauty, in dollars and cents, to a town like ours. I would save that great and beautiful tree!

"Is that elm tree on public property?" asked the tree warden.

I had to confess at once that it was not. It was close to the line, but it was on private property. I did not need to be told how hopeless the case was; there are few things more sacred to us in New England than private property: the right of a man to do what he will with his own. I had a satisfying example of this characteristic the other day when I walked uptown with my neighbor, Carpenter. There is a cut-across that saves a number of steps. Carpenter followed around by the sidewalk. When I commented upon it, he said:

"Well, I don't want anyone cutting across my ground, and so, by jinx, I won't cross any other man's ground."

The land is unoccupied, and practically everyone cuts across, but, by jinx, C. won't, even though he makes the trip four times every day.

I now dreaded the worst, but day after day passed, and the woodsman did not appear. I learned by grapevine telegraph that the old man had been forced to delay. He had found that the cutting and working up of such a great tree was a veritable engineering operation, and the cost of it at least temporarily prohibitive. But who could tell when his wrath might overcome every other consideration?

I had still one other difficult resource, and I acted

upon it. Through the good offices of a friend, I was finally able to purchase outright the meadow where the tree stands. It is now, of course, no more my elm tree than it was before; it really belongs to any and all casual travelers with the gift for spiritual possession— but I now hold the silly bit of paper which makes me at once the arbiter and the sharer of the noblest tree in the countryside.

We have had one more period of sharp anxiety. This was during the great hurricane of 1938, the first in the history of the valley, which smote our town with unbelievable ferocity. Many of the finest trees in all our valley, probably half of the giant elms which gave beauty and dignity to our streets, were ruthlessly destroyed. We watched the storm sweeping across the hills; we saw the great boughs of our elm, so long the pattern of strength and serenity, begin to sway and beat about in the storm as though in an agony of fear. They seemed literally to turn over; twisting wildly; and the green leaves, stripped loose, were sent whirling up the valley. It did not seem possible that the tree could stand. One branch of considerable size, indeed, was torn away, and so fierce was the wind that it was driven across the open land, seventy or eighty feet, to tear through one of the windows of our home.

And yet it stood. It stood! The next morning, there in the bright sunshine, it lifted itself skyward, as serenely majestic as ever. Other trees by hundreds had gone down, our elm scarcely showed a scratch. Looking up at it that morning, one found his eyes grow misty with pride and sympathy and relief.

Old elm, I knew why you stood! I knew why the greatest hurricane ever known in all our country could not put you down. It was because you had grown in open spaces. You had been pruned and toughened and disciplined by the storms of a century. You had put your great gnarled roots down into the strong soil of New England. Stout old individualist!—you grew in no supporting forest environment; you had known no pampering; you were as strong on your south as on your north, on your west as on your east; you had room, old pioneer, and you used it to grow in. When the storm blew, and the flood came, you stood! You stood, stanch centenarian, to live your life and delight your time.

So many people that day in the town asked me first of all, when we met, knowing how much I loved my elm:

"Did your tree stand?" or doubtfully, "How did your elm come through?"

What a satisfaction to quiet the solicitude of the town! Never again, looking up into those leafy depths where the orioles nest and the robins sing, shall I forget the thrill I felt that morning when I saw with what sturdy courage the old giant still held the long purpose.

I thought in the early years that our elm was older than the recorded settlement of the town by white men.

I thought of it as standing there, a living thing, long before New England marched with George Washington, perhaps as old as the landing of the *Mayflower* on the rocky coast of Massachusetts.

But when I began to make inquiries of men who had studied the age of trees in the valley, and had myself counted the rings on several other huge old trees that had been blown down, I came to the conclusion that it was not much above a hundred years old. The elms of Hadley and Amherst were probably planted between 1815 and 1840. My elm, I think, was never planted by the hand of man but grew, a chance seedling in the hedge along the rail fence that separated the old Smith farm, part of which we now own, and the land of the Cutlers.

It seems no larger than it was when we first saw it, over thirty years ago. Elms grow rapidly in their youth and hold long to their maturity. Tom Smith, who grew up on the Smith farm, told me that he remembered the elm in his boyhood, fifty years ago, and it seemed as large then as it is now. I have helped it as well as I knew by fertilizing the land around it two or three times in recent years, though I doubt whether this did any real good. At any rate, it now seems hale and hearty for one of its age.

My elm is the true patriarch of our hillside: the progenitor of an innumerable family. There must be hundreds, if not thousands, of its descendants in the hedge-

rows and woodlots of the neighborhood. Walking out
the other day, I saw in the road, where the rain had
recently fallen, heavy windrows, washed up like sea-
weed left by the surf, of the seeds of the great tree.
There were masses of the round, tan-colored, glabrous
fruits that could have been gathered up in great hand-
fuls—bushels of them. As I looked further, I found them
thickly strewn across many square rods of the meadow,
brought down no doubt by the rain. They had washed
or been blown into cracks of the walk, chinked into
crevices of the porches of the house, cunningly scattered, as I looked to see, among the shrubs and border
plantings all about. What a sowing! It was inconceivable. There must have been many thousands, if not
millions, of seeds from that one tree. What a struggle
for perpetuity! What a gambler's fling for immortality!
And yet of all of this enormous spermal prodigality, will
a single seed, in these well-controlled gardens and
meadows and hedgerows, find a chance to germinate
and grow?—let alone produce another elm tree a hundred years old?

I myself have pulled elm trees out of my grape bor-
ders and shrub beds between my thumb and finger. Elm
trees—weeds! This very spring, after consideration, I
cut short the life of a promising descendant of my elm,
even though I had come to have a kind of love for it. It
had sprouted close to an old fence, where, in the secrecy
of nature, the seed had been cunningly dropped. I did

not see it until it had been growing for two or three years, possibly longer. There it was, struggling upward cheerfully among a tangle of grass and woodbine. I thought of the possibilities of that small seedling wrestling now with petty and short-lived competitors, but destined, if fate willed, to outlast uncounted generations of the grass, unnumbered flowerings of the woodbine, to grow immeasurably larger than any of them, a veritable marvel of the countryside. I watched it for two or three years with growing interest, and a kind of affection, and presently I brought down my pruning shears, cut away some of the entanglement about it, and sheared the lower branches, that it might speedily have a better chance to grow. In a year or so it was higher than my head and as thrifty as you please, for its roots reached out on both sides into the cultivated land. This spring, however, we made some new plans for our garden and orchard which involved the removal of the old fence and the tangled hedgerow in which the young elm was growing. At first I could not think of cutting it away. But it did not fit into the Plan. I thought of moving it, but there was no place anywhere upon our hillside where we wanted an elm tree; and to move it would have robbed it of that peculiar virtue of survival by struggle with which it had taken hold of my interest. So finally, the Plan being immutable, I cut it out.

Considering all these things today, I am newly thrilled by the majestic tranquillity of my elm. How it

stands there glorious in the sun; how it takes the rain!
It has cast a billion seeds. Will any grow? It is content.
It does not weep with remorse over its past, nor tremble
for its future. It flings its loveliness to the sky, it is content with spring; it is glorious in summer; it is patient
through the long winter.

Birds I Have Known

VIII

Birds I Have Known

I HAVE BEEN wanting to write about some of the birds I have known. I am no ornithologist; I know really very little scientifically about them. Many varieties, not uncommon even here in this valley, I do not easily recognize, and I have none of the ability a friend of mine possesses in such generous measure (so that I envy him) of distinguishing birds by mere fragments of their songs. Yet I have here and there in my life met birds—a bird here and there—when I was in a moment of intense living. These I shall never forget. They have meant something strange, or deep, or beautiful to me.

I cannot say I love birds—miscellaneously. I cannot say I love men—mankind—miscellaneously. I see him too vividly; there is far too much and too many of him; it spreads me out too thin. I think I can say honestly that I am *interested* in all men: I wonder about them; I like to look at them; I enjoy hearing or reading about them, whether they are of this age or another; but there are only a few men here and there whom I have met with the full intensity of life and have therefore come to love. So also it is with the birds.

I saw this very morning—this gray November morning—the first black-capped chickadees of the year, at least on this hillside. They blessed my eyes and cleansed my soul. One of the cheerfulest of birds, eager, fearless, busy, and beyond description graceful in all of their little swift flights. One of them was exploring the riches of a woodsy plantation of goldenrod not far from the roadside, now brown with autumn, withered leaves, and feathery gray plumes where the yellow blossoms had been. I stood a long time to watch, thinking it one of the most pleasing sights that ever I saw in my life—how the little bird ran up the stalks, plunging into and shaking the fluffy dry flowers, running down again, evidently to retrieve seeds that had fallen into the axil of the dead leaves, sometimes even darting down to the ground, where its sharp eyes had discovered treasures I myself could not see. How brilliantly black its busy topknot and the spots on its throat; how vivid the white parts of its head! Exquisitely alive, active, free—beyond the art of man!—possible only to Nature at her utmost.

I think it wonderful of a morning to come upon such a sight: I have enjoyed it all day.

I think I can best speak of a few other such meetings by using the notes I made at the time, while the experiences were still warm in my mind.

TREE SPARROWS

JANUARY 27. Upon my windowsill, at this moment, not above three feet from my hand as I write, there are a half-dozen jaunty little tree sparrows pecking at the breakfast food I scattered there an hour ago. The sound of their bills upon the wood is like the dropping of rain. Such cheerful little balls of brown and gray feathers I never saw; such playful, quarrelsome little rascals. The table is big enough for them all, but no more than two or three can eat at a time for very jealousy. All night they hide among the branches of the spruce trees behind drifts of snow and are here on hand as early as I am, at dawn, to get their breakfast. What a joy they are in a torn world!

JUNCOS

APRIL 7. Juncos are unusually plentiful this spring. I have seen many large flocks about the meadows and along the roadsides—very cheerful in their slate-gray coats and fresh white vests. I spent some time today watching them. One habit they have I had not before closely observed. The two white feathers in the tail are not ordinarily noticeable when they are at rest, but they have a habit, when alarmed, of so spreading their tails that these feathers flash white, and they are off in an instant. They are friendly, sociable birds, and even their rather inconspicuous chirp or *chip* is pleasing these early spring days.

BLUE JAYS

FEBRUARY 10. Sunshine and soft warmth. The heavy snow is melting. As I walked through the near-by woods I saw a blue jay very joyful, crying "jay, jay, jay"— three sharp notes often repeated. The jay hardly appears to fly: he, rather, flashes. Though an unpopular bird, because he is like some men who have a sharp brilliancy of appearance coupled with a harsh or witty tongue, I rather like him. He is an ardent, daring, encouraging bird. "Do it," he seems always to say, "do it, do it, do it." He remains with us all winter long, hiding in the thick branches of the spruces or squatting in the low, dense shrubbery. He is quiet enough during cold weather, but on the first day like this out he comes, as jaunty and confident as you please, ready to take early advantage of any opportunity that may present itself. My friend, the ornithologist, tells me that the jay will even begin nest building on warm days in January—pulling apart his old nest, preparatory to new construction. He has many curious notes besides the "jay, jay, jay" of this time of year. Indeed, he is often imitative of other birds, especially of the evening cry of one of the small hawks. One cry in particular he seems unable to utter unless he bends his knees, squats down, and then suddenly rises again, the cry bursting from his beak. He is not a very wise bird. He continues to nest in the spruce trees where the squirrels go for cones—and take his eggs and young ones. The robin has learned the lesson of the spruce tree! Complete monogamy appears to exist among the jays: once married, married for life. And it is difficult to distinguish outwardly male from female: both appear to sit on the eggs. Equality of the sexes; is that, in the long run, the result of monogamy? The polygamous birds—fowls, grouse, turkeys, and the like—develop larger males—for fighting. Like mankind.

I've seen the jays stealing corn from field shocks in the winter, taking a grain at a time and worrying it down into pieces by pecking it. Otherwise they do not injure agricultural crops, save as they destroy useful and insect-eating birds. But like all life that lives by blood, the jay also dies by blood: all other birds are against him and destroy him and his young remorselessly, so that he does not increase rapidly.

BROWN THRASHER

I think certainly I should say something of the brown thrasher, an old friend much loved these many years. A pair has nested in a thicket of prickly barberries west of the house. They are shy birds, expert runners and skulkers, but mornings like these, when the maples are beginning to bloom, they sing from the topmost branches, a flood of joy, the high sweet poetry of spring. . . .

WRENS

He who shall hurt the little wren
Shall never be beloved by men.

A delightful thing: the wrens building now in our little green house; dainty visitors for several days, they have become our permanent tenants. . . .

The incessant wren! A pleasant song, soon too much. Another bird that presently wearies is the Maryland yellowthroat, like the monotony of the cicada in the heat of summer and that of the cricket in the cool of early fall. The song sparrow is also a persistent singer, but she never wearies, but contents, but allures. At noon the sparrow on the housetop!

HERMIT THRUSH

OCTOBER 14. We have had a shy visitor, in olive brown coat and a cravat of polka dots. I heard him first at the west door, and when I tiptoed to see, there he was, clinging to a sprig of the woodbine, among the autumn-red leaves. He was having his breakfast, as much at home as you please, on the purple, ripe berries. A hermit thrush, one of the choicest of all our birds. At the right time of the year there is no finer or sweeter singer. I crept close and looked at him long and carefully. His colors are duller this fall than earlier. . . .

Bluebirds, hermit thrushes, robins, myrtle warblers, all are now visiting my window for the purple berries of the creeper.

BALTIMORE ORIOLES

MAY 15. In the space of ten minutes, early this morning, I saw two Baltimore orioles (the first of the spring); catbirds, which are nesting almost at my window in the barberries (a bird I love); bobolinks; meadow larks; a jay; crows being chased by a kingbird, which is now the undesired tyrant of my orchard and preys upon the bees; and finally the robins, which have a nest in the euonymus.

A DAY WITH THE BIRDS

SUNDAY, APRIL 19. Long walk in the woods. Bright, clear day, though so windy that many of the birds were not out. My ornithologist friend was with me, both forenoon and afternoon.

We saw two birds we have never seen here before. They were in the wet corner of our own field, and my friend identified them as Wilson's snipes. They flew off quickly in a swift zigzagging rush with a kind of wild cry. I saw plainly their long beaks and large eyes. They dropped again among tussocks of grass in the marsh lot and utterly disappeared—until I was almost on them. They hide wonderfully. Then up they rose again and repeated the swift flight and sudden alighting further away. We also saw a number of beautiful myrtle warblers—newly here—and among them a few olive-colored birds with russet topknots which we looked up when we got home and think them the redpoll warbler.

We saw also:

Robins which are just finishing their nests; some have begun to lay.

Many crows, flying in pairs, brood far along.

White-bellied swallows among the swamp willows.

Killdeer flashing along the fields near the low, watered meadows.

Vesper sparrow or grass finch which I, with the ornithologist's help, identified for the first time. Its song is sweet, but I do not like it as well as that of the song sparrow, of which we heard many.

Meadow lark, only one seen.

No catbirds or yellow warblers (which I called summer yellowbird when a boy). Apparently they are not yet here.

Downy and hairy woodpeckers.

Chewink or ground robin.

Three kinds of blackbirds: crow blackbird, red-shouldered, and rusty; all in the marshes or near them.

Cowbird, the rascal.

Junco or snowbird, now nesting.

Hermit thrush, that gleam in the deep woods.

There are plenty of blue jays about, but we saw not one. The martins have come to the martin houses.

TERMITES FOR BREAKFAST

JANUARY 10. We are on a visit to Florida, and I have just spent a wholly absorbed and delightful hour watching a flock of unfamiliar birds that I thought at first were flycatchers. They were engaged in the interesting and urgent business of getting their breakfast. Part of them were in the orange trees and part on the roof of the porch, and the field of their activity was the sunny air between. Never have I seen more bewildering and thrilling flights and forays. This flycatcher is a little fellow, not more than four or five inches long, I should think, with a sharp bill, a brilliant eye, a bib of mottled brown, a perky little tail, rather long, and a single black spot on the rump. He gives a general impression of brown and tan, although in some of his flights he displays, or seems to display, flashes of blue or green. I have been unable to identify him positively, even in my dependable little book—I know too little of the birds even at home, how much less in Florida!—but this did not at all disturb my enjoyment. Innumerable small flies, seemingly just hatched, were rising from the steaming earth into the clear air. While they had a protective eccentricity in their flight, it did not prevent the eager little flycatchers from capturing them literally by the hundreds. Again and again I saw a single bird in its astonishing flight between the orange trees and the porch roof—darting, curving, rising, swooping, faster, almost, than the eye could follow—take as many as a dozen flies, apparently swallowing them instantly on the wing. One little fellow, however, seemed to prefer to remain on the roof edge and dart out as the flies arose, catching one unerringly each time. Once or twice I saw him hold a fly for an instant in his bill before swallowing it. Evidently he was a little more of the epicure! There must have been a dozen or more birds in the flock, but there seemed an inexhaustible number of flies. I had great enjoyment of this spectacle—not only the flight of the birds, but the high blue of the sky, the sunshine, the blooming bougainvillaea, and in the distance, the gleaming water of the little lake. A fine moment of life! For everyone except the flies!

I continued on other days to watch this drama of the sunny mornings; but I found that the "flies" I saw had *four* wings and knew that they could not, therefore, properly be called flies. And when I talked with our expert on Florida birds, I made the discovery that my "flycatcher" was not a flycatcher at all—but a palm warbler. And the "flies" are termites swarming from the warm earth—probably from colonies that are now engaged in silently but effectively eating up this house. It all shows how careful a man must be, in an unfamiliar country, in the use of his words. One must know his termites!

BIRD AND MOTH

JUNE 15. I saw a catbird today playing with a small white moth, like a cat with a mouse, letting it go, only to seize it again instantly when it tried to fly.

A MOCKINGBIRD IN NEW ENGLAND

SUNDAY, FEBRUARY 14. A rare visitor. Looking out our window to the vine where we have placed a piece of suet for the birds, we saw the rarest sight of its kind that ever blessed our eyes. We have had plenty of chickadees, jays, and tree sparrows, and once a whooping flock of starlings—but today we saw a *mockingbird*. I never knew that they visited us even in summer, let alone winter. We had already heard—with doubt—from a neighbor that a mockingbird had been seen upon this hillside, but had no idea of getting a glimpse of it. I thought at first it was a catbird, but a winter catbird is unknown here. They are even late in coming in the spring. Moreover, this was a shorter, stockier bird, with quite different markings, as we could see plainly, being only a dozen feet away. It gave us great joy.

(It was undoubtedly a mockingbird: I have made inquiries of local bird authorities in the state. They have been seen here before in the winter.)

We Go Fishing

IX

We Go Fishing

IT WAS in the morning that my friend Waugh called me up.

"How about going trout fishing tomorrow?"

Many a year, near the beginning of the apple blossoms, when the New England hillsides are at their best, Waugh and I have been going fishing.

It gave me a curious thrill, but my first instinctive impulse was to say no. How stop work for a full day? Had I not promised myself five pages of copy for the printer? Did not my garden demand immediate attention; might not my bees go off in swarms for want of proper spring management?

"No," said I. "Too busy. Can't go."

"The hills will never be better," commented Waugh beguilingly. "The shadbush is in bloom."

"But——" said I.

"Barrus says the trout are really rising," said Waugh.

"But——" said I.

"We can take along the old frying pan."

I had felt myself slipping. I think it was the old frying pan, and the vision of a luncheon cooked in the woods, that was my undoing.

"I'm your man," said I. "Let's go! What's work anyhow?"

All that day at my desk I heard something singing away back in the dusky places of the mind. We were going fishing! When I read in the morning papers of the woes of a turbulent world, I said to myself, "Never mind; we're going fishing." When I thought of the war in China and the dire confusion of Europe, my mind slipped aside to remembered glimpses of swift-running sunny water, and I in hip boots, flecking the pools with a choice Montreal or a Parmachene Belle.

That afternoon, as soon as I could get a moment of free time, I went up to the corner of the attic where I keep my fishing togs. I got out my best rod and fitted it together, making sure that it was in perfect condition. I looked over and sorted my flies. Were there leaders enough? And where was my small canvas creel? And my old fishing coat with the roomy pockets?

If you are not a fisherman, you do not know the thrill of wetting up the felt pads in a leader box and putting half a dozen leaders to soak. You cannot quite imagine the joy of choosing just the flies, just the size of hooks, for such an early May trip to the Goshen Hills.

I took quite a superior delight in replying to everybody and anybody who wanted me to do anything on
Friday:

"Can't do it, going fishing."

Every time I said it I felt somehow freer and happier.
Among our hills it is a well-understood and thoroughly
accepted excuse. It is as though one said, "Sorry. Can't.
Getting married tomorrow." If I had argued, "I'm too
busy, all tied up, work won't let me off," I should merely
have been regarded with suspicion, and subjected to renewed pressure. But fishing. . . .

Friday morning proved absolutely perfect: all sunshine, with little soft breezes from the south. And here
was I in my soiled fishing coat, my shapeless old hat; and
here was Waugh coming out to meet me with a broad
smile on his face, his rucksack on his shoulder and his
rods and his boots in his hands. It was a reality. It was
going to happen. We were off for a day in the hills.

In our country, fishing is one of the permitted joys. I
think it always evaded the dour old puritan suspicion of
joy, or happiness, or pleasure. For when spring steals
into our valley after the long winter, who can resist it?
There is, indeed, an earlier joy: the maple sugar season
—buckets on the trees, the steamy sap houses, hot syrup
sugared off in a pail of snow; but that is an aimed and
labored joy, with a reward to satisfy the conscience even
of a seasoned Yankee. Something that can be sold afterward! But fishing? Two strong men toiling all day long

among the brush and fallen logs, sloshing through ice-cold water, and coming in at night tired and happy, with a few ounces of little fish. It is one of the grandly humorous jokes of New England. No, there is no excuse for fishing except joy.

In the valley the apple trees were beginning to blossom; on the hills we were among the first glories of the spring woods. The shadbush was a white mist upon the woody hillsides. The earlier spicebush, with its gleam of gold, was passing, but the fragrant sassafras, especially on southern slopes, was at its best. Here and there in old fields we saw the ruddy spring glow of the high-bush huckleberries, and along the hedges and the fences the pin cherries, with their neatly rounded blossom clusters, were beginning to come out. I think no moment of the year is like this, so disturbingly beautiful.

We walked down the hill by an old wood road, crossed an opening where in times past there had been a sawmill—a weathered brown dune of sawdust still marked the spot—and came at last to the brook near the end of an antiquated and broken-down loggers' bridge. The swift-rushing stream had been partially dammed by the obstructions, and a little still pond above the old bridge reflected the clear morning sky, and a fleecy cloud or two, and the trees. The water poured through the crude planking and rushed noisily among great boulders just below. One's eye chose instantly the pool into which to cast the first fly—just above the timbers, where it would drift artfully downward to the dark waters where the mythical big one was sure to be lurking. It was as pleasant a scene as any fisher could desire. So we sat down there on the brookside in the sunshine to joint our rods, thread through the line from the reel, and choose, after some discussion, the little dark fly best suited to the earliness of the season. Then we strapped up our boots, fitted our canvas creels to our shoulders, and were ready for the fray.

(I may say in confidence that we had brought with us also a sufficient supply of lifesaving worms. For if the trout refused to rise to our flies, we were prepared with a menu better adapted to their delicate appetites.)

The perfections of a New England trout brook! Hills above clad with birches and great old hemlocks, ferns crowding so near the water that their fronds dipped in, the stream itself full of old round boulders, and pools, and eddies, and delightful little gravel bars where one could stand to cast into the stream below. And the music of it all, and the sunshine of a morning in May. . . .

To a man mewed up in a study so much of every day, this logger's job of climbing slippery boulders, straddling fallen logs, wading through tricky shallows, with the swift water sucking at one's boots, this exertion on a warm morning, was considerable. Presently I sat down on a mossy bank to rest a bit. I forgot to say that I was alone—as a man ought to be when he approaches the really momentous events of life—for Waugh chose to fish up the stream and I down it, with an agreement to meet later.

It is a deep valley the stream runs through. Both sides are heavily wooded. Among the undergrowth are great clumps of mountain laurel not yet in bloom, and hobblebush and dogwood. On all sides were the delicate uncurling fronds of a small variety of wood fern, charming to see. As I sat there listening to the infinitely calming music of the stream rushing over its shining stones, I heard away off in the deep woods the reedy trill of a hermit thrush. Nothing I know, in all the wild places of the hills, has in it so much of the mystery, the beauty, the veritable spirit of the place as the note of the hermit thrush.

So I sat there for some time. All the complications and cares of life seemed to have slipped away. I was content.

(When I left home on Friday morning I had put aside several knotty problems. I had put them away in the warm deep places of the mind. While I was not looking, that day on Barrus Brook, the sunshine somehow got into them, and the clear air, and the music of the water among the stones—and the blossoming shadbushes, and the birds—and when the next morning I had my problems out again, there they were, quite clear and simple, no more perplexities.)

Presently, being thirsty, I began to look around me, and I soon found a little rivulet flowing down the hillside among ferns and wintergreen, among the moss and the old roots of the trees. Just before it made its last long leap into the brook it paused for a moment in a kind of adolescent pool, small and so still that it reflected a bit of the sky. Standing there in the brook itself, I leaned over and drank from the edge of the little pool, cold, clear water fresh from the earth itself.

It was comforting to have my faith in myself confirmed, for at nearly every likely pool I had a strike at the first cast, though the fish, plainly too well fed by the high water of the spring, were not so voracious as one could wish. And, unlike the streams I knew so well as a boy, it was stocked by a benevolent state and then fished out before the poor little fingerlings had a chance to grow to maturity, so that many of the trout caught were undersize and had to be thrown back. (A comment on the times! A benevolent state pouring out its lavish beneficences, and individuals unwilling to restrain themselves.) Nevertheless, I was lured always onward, always there was a more inviting pool just below. And the joy of fishing, as any real fisherman knows, does not consist merely in the number of fish taken.

Near a branch of Barrus Brook there is an old sugar-house, in March the center of the farmer's activity, for there the maple sap is boiled down, but for the remainder of the year the place is deserted, the home of the chipmunk, and wild bees and wasps, and possibly a porcupine or a woodchuck. Here in an open space

Waugh and I have sometimes cooked our luncheon. A spring is near at hand, where an old-fashioned cracked iron syrup kettle has been sunk into the earth and holds for a moment the water of a spring from the hill above. Here we build our little fire—an Indian fire with as few sticks and twigs as possible—and here Waugh squats down with the frying pan to cook the bacon and fry a few of the fish we have caught. This is one of the high moments of any well-regulated fishing trip—the baiting of the fishers themselves.

So we sit there in the still woods to eat our luncheon, declaring our conviction that no fish known to man has a finer flavor than the brook trout. We drink from tin cups dipped in the spring. We discuss the events of the forenoon—all the big ones we lost—and plan in detail for what is yet to come. We discuss also the wild things of the woods, which Waugh knows not only by their proper and dignified titles, but by their familiar and intimate names. He thinks that human beings, in competition with their creations, are shrinking in stature and significance (though not from modesty), and that they travel too fast, these days, to know or love the quiet beauties of the woods.

"At forty miles an hour," says Waugh, "one cannot see any more violets. About all he can recognize is an apple tree in full bloom. And when we change from automobiles to airplanes, it will require a whole orchard to catch the eye."

But there is a possible remedy in sight.

"Perhaps," says Waugh, "if man shrinks enough, he will again find the violets."

Of all the experiences and sensations of the day, none is more delightful than the well-earned weariness at the end of it. Not nervous, not mental, but that delightful sense of physical fatigue which steals over a man's body, soothing and relaxing. The ride through the woods in the cool of the evening, supper at home with an appetite one has not had for weeks, and early afterward to bed. . . .

This it is to go fishing with Waugh.

Things I Delight In

X

Things I Delight In

AN OLD PASTURE in spring, all silence and sunshine, I love well, and the bluets and the dandelions that grow there, and the alders and willows that hedge the low spots. All this I love well.

The shadbush is in bloom on Pelham Road, and in my garden, daffodils and poets' narcissus. The Chinese magnolias are lustrous in many a pampered garden.

I am never less alone than when I am alone. . . .

How gladly I return to "my woodlands and my little farm that restore me to myself," as Horace said.

It is a beautiful thing, past expression, to be here on my own hillside, on such a morning in June. To be *alive* here!

I sat a long time in my sunny garden. I forget from spring to spring, I forget that there can be such days, and such beauty. I remember, as a *fact*, that there are miracles; I forget that they are forever being new-wrought, every year new-wrought, as though in all time they had never been before. I forget how they are transmuted, all living, into the soul of a man.

I have no proper words to tell of what I saw and felt there in my garden—the surprise, the newness, of the way of a thrush in a thicket, the way of ferns in the crevices of old walls.

I saw Mother Bumblebee visiting the bloom of the tall white clematis, and a hummingbird—morsel of animate rainbow, quite unbelievable in its magic, if I had not been there to see—among the yellow foxgloves and purple larkspurs. (This hummingbird visiting the larkspur began always at the bottom of the blossoms and worked upward.) And the wind in the pine tops and the pattern of the ivy on the wall. . . .

A heavy fog this autumn morning, clearing away to give us a day of brilliant sunshine and heat. I worked hard all forenoon at my desk and spent this afternoon in my old clothes, mostly in my garden.

Bees are now on the purple asters, bees and vacillating yellow butterflies in the sunny air; the goldenrod is passing; seeds are falling from the heavy-headed sunflowers; the walnuts are coming down. I see clusters of brilliant red berries on the dogwoods, and the Jonathan apple trees are borne low with fruit. In my field, long

brown rows of ripe onions and bags of harvested
potatoes.

> *How miracles abound*
> *In each small plot of ground.*

The richest enjoyment, especially of nature, comes
with complete self-forgetfulness, as this morning when
I walked in my garden and never knew until afterward
that I was happy. Time and space forgot! No gnawing
anxiety of the common day.

I have just introduced a new Italian queen in No. 4
colony of my apiary, the old queen appearing bedrag-
gled, with little brood-laying. I saw her twice this spring,
but today I could not find her at all, even though I
went through the frames three times. Negative knowledge is deceptive, but I put in her ladyship, the new
queen, just as she arrived in her little wire cage with
three or four of her faithful courtiers about her. I hope
for the best. [MAY 18. The colony accepted her.]

The spring is coming gloriously. The Wealthy and
Gravenstein apples are blooming; we sprayed the first
time two days ago. Our pink dogwoods are a sight for
jaundiced eyes. Tulips are now opening, the forsythia
and shadbush passing. The huge Judas tree in Mrs.
C.'s yard is at its purple best.

Up early these days to work in quietude. This is
smoky autumn, half asleep, serene with bountiful

harvests. I have one Northern Spy apple tree that has just come into bearing. Today I picked the crop: a scant basket, but magnificent great apples, perfect to the last pale blush. They are poor yielders in this neighborhood, but next February one will go far to find a better apple.

I have been swimming the last two days—just at evening. It is the finest and best of all exercises, and the most enjoyable. To plunge into a still lake and swim straight out into the cool water after a day of intense heat is one of the most delightful things a man can do. To turn over lazily in the water, to look up at the hills, to watch the fleecy clouds in the sky, and the far flight of birds in the high air. To lie there floating with the water whispering gently at one's ear and then to turn again to strong deep strokes. . . .

Quietly at work all this afternoon, making up hundreds of comb-honey sections, and neatly fitting in the starters, setting all compactly in the supers. I like the look of the clean white wood, and the smell of it; I like every deft process of my hands.

In the hot evening I saw a little tousle-headed boy with a cane fish pole on his shoulder. Shirttail out, grimy bare toes, but a glowing face, for he carried a string of half a dozen little yellow perch. Not so long ago I myself was that boy!

[180]

THINGS I DELIGHT IN

On a May morning:

Newly plowed, warm, wet fields smoking after the rain.

A kingbird, hovering, then darting like a swift arrow, to capture one of my honeybees.

A little grubby boy wiping his red nose by a vigorous push upward with the palm of his hand.

A good neighbor woman, the Argus-eyed reporter of our neighborhood, seeing me walking on my hillside, says I am loafing. . . .

Fame. Today, walking in the autumn woods, a maple leaf fell on my hat. I picked it off and held it in my hand. I noted the marvelous beauty of its inner tracery, the richness of its coloring, the utter perfection of its form. Out of a billion billion leaves in the forest, this one alone had fallen on my hat; this alone I had taken in my hand to wonder at. It was not finer or more beautiful than the billion billion others—but it had fallen on my hat.

JANUARY 1. Just at sunset I went out with my wedges, ax, and sledge to the log pile. It was sharp, clear, very cold. A few ragged clouds, dead gray and mournful with the winter, filled the horizon to the north. The dead white fields hardly softened the dreary brown hills, and brown trees stretched toward the sunset. It was still and very cold. The snow complained under my feet, and my breath was a frosty plume. So I cut a notch in the end of the elm block, put in my wedge, and drove it down with the sledge. How the steel rang on the steel!

And at sunset, the gray, ragged clouds were reddened for a moment with a halfhearted glow, and then the cold and gloom deepened; and a thin pale moon came out in the high heavens, scudding through the clouds, and one by one the lights of Plainville and South Deerfield pricked through the dark wall of the distant hills. And as I worked there in the biting cold, the gray weariness of the earth closed in around me and rested heavy upon my heart. Oh, that I knew where I might find Him!

A Chronicle of Small Joys

XI

A Chronicle of Small Joys

1. THE DAILY NEWSPAPER

FEBRUARY 2. This day breaks clear and cool: such sunshine as would make gods or angels envious.

Thinking of my days, how pleasant, how sweet are certain unconsidered moments. This morning, after my coffee, which I make now in a new way, most delicious, and drink with no cream and little sugar, so that I taste the rare flavor of the good coffee itself—this morning, after my coffee, I sat down in a chair by the sunny window and opened the morning paper on my knee. How pleasant it was to look over the headlines concerning the distant and unreal world, all the kidnapings and murders, and lynchings and suicides!—and how President Roosevelt had received 200,000 birthday greetings and had devalued the dollar to sixty cents, how a Senator had caned a newspaper reporter (wherein I could not decide which had my sympathy), and that there was two feet of snow in Washington, which made

me wholly content. I read of a prima donna and reflected that it would be impossible to call a prima donna
anything but Madame or to allow her to occupy anything in a hotel but a suite, and so on to the little news
of the town, whereupon I gloated upon all of the teas
and dinners I did not have to attend, and the lectures I
could escape listening to.

All this I lived through in a few minutes and knew
that I had enjoyed myself. A delightful interlude before
sitting down at my desk. I think it is not the occupations
of life, of which these common moments are sometimes
the best, but the empty interludes that annoy us most.
We are bored not by living but by not living.

2. A SUNDAY MORNING

MAY 30. Sunday morning again, and blessed rest. A
warm, still spring day with all the world blooming.
Soft airs all about and blessed quietude. I am visiting
my old, old friend, the oak, who provides me a seat
among its mighty gnarled roots where they take hold
of the soil. It is cushioned with dry, dead leaves and
grass and squawberry vines, and the edges of the
cushion are well trimmed with the lace of gay fern
leaves. Here I rest. I look out into the green depths
of the still woods, new beech and maple leaves with
darker hemlocks interspersed. A moment ago the alarm
of the forest sounded, splitting the silence. The clamor
of crows.

"Dumb woods, hast uttered a bird?"

I saw just now a cardinal bird—flame of the wood.

How it escapes one—the spring. It will not stay. We love it and it vanishes.

3. A CAT IN A WINDOW

MAY 10. I wondered today, walking slowly along the road, how it was that so many simple things give me such exquisite joy. I saw a gray cat curled on a window ledge in the morning sun, and stood looking at her with such a sense of *fitness*, such an understanding of comfort, as I cannot describe. Why should a cat in a window please me? Why should I *care* to stand and watch her there luxuriating in the sun? Why should I recall the experience for several days afterward with a warm sense of remembered delight?

4. I AM IMPATIENT THESE DAYS

I am impatient these days: there is not time enough in this one life. I need more lives; I have made plans already for three or four. I could easily expand to ten or twenty, all full-flavored, ardent, interesting. Full of curiosity! Looking into the sciences one after another, traveling to unexplored places, not only geographical, but psychological, social, economic; reading all the good books I do not yet know, and in all the languages; meeting every interesting human being then alive and with leisure—with leisure!—to know, to talk, to love.

And to write! Time to write, and having written, to rewrite. I have enjoyed this earth; the only flaw is that my time here is too short.

5. PLOWING AT NIGHT

JUNE 20. Tractor of our neighbors of the Colomont farm throbbing half the hot moonlit night. I walk over to see what they are doing; they are driving their work hard. I have never before seen a tractor fitted with a headlight upon it for plowing at night. They are breaking up the old marshland. These youths! These youths! Working day and night.

I know, deep down (being old, or nearly old) that they will not find all they seek; they will not get riches, or security; they will not get all the happiness they look forward to—but this does not distress me, or make me sour about life. I think to myself: what a time these youths are having! What wonders they are achieving! For they are enjoying themselves *now*, living *now*, working *now*.

6. YANKEE FARMER

An improvident Yankee farmer I know drives the most marvelous contraption of an old wagon that ever I saw. I wonder sometimes how he ever gets anywhere with it, but he seems actually to like it. I think it piques the native ingenuity with which he is so abundantly blessed. Whenever a whippletree breaks, or a lug pulls out, or a tire slips he shifts his tobacco from one cheek to the other and with a nail, a bit of haywire, and a stone he soon makes all as good as before. He's a wonder at tinkering, that farmer. When he gets in again, he exclaims, "Thar, by gosh"—and you feel a solid confidence that somehow he's going to get to town.

Well, that's America. We're great tinkerers, love to employ our ingenuity in patching our ancient and inefficient wagons—and, somehow, we always get to town.

7. SITTING AT MY WINDOW, WRITING

MARCH 13. I was up at dawn this misty spring morning, and as I sat here at my window, writing, I saw in glances the slow daybreak. There was rain in the night, and all the delicate twigs of the spiraea at my window are pearled with drops of water. I can see the eastern light gleaming among them, so that they look as hard and cold-white as frost crystals. And all around me these quiet morning hours lie my books and papers: just here at my left the musty records I am working upon; my notebooks there; the half-shaped clay of my chapters lying in a semicircle at my elbow, where I can give a pat to this paragraph or strike a bit of unnecessary mud from that. And there stands my friendly familiar, with his comfortable potbelly, his bald head, and his air of worldly wisdom—My Ink Bottle; and here in the open case my everyday spectacles, ready so that if anyone comes in, I can quickly and secretly slip them on and make believe I don't need reading glasses. Near at hand is my old friend with his two-faced duplicity, my Calendar, who tells me how time flies and that if I do not hurry I shall be old before my work is done. And here are my bookcases—not an arm's length away—where I can find anything I want—almost anything!—but what I can't find is sometimes infuriating.

Is there anything in the world better than this? Here is where I live: this is my joy. I shall never have any reward better than this.

8. MY NOTEBOOK

I should like my writing to appear to be exactly what it is—as though I had just stepped in, excited, from the fields, eager to put down what I have heard or seen or felt or thought.

The beauty of a notebook is that it need not be final —everything fresh, immediate, unfinished, like life itself. No conclusions: glimpses. Sometimes I run down in the middle of a sentence and stop with a dash. I suspect periods, but I like commas and semicolons, since they imply that there is still much to be said. I know I use too many exclamation points, but the fact is, I am so astonished by some of the things I see and hear of a spring morning that it is only an exclamation point that will relieve my feelings!

I have a beautiful idea on page 36, I doubt it on

page 42, change it beyond recognition on page 110—
and on page 303, having entirely forgotten what I said
before, re-express it as a beautiful idea in terms exactly
similar to those on page 36. Which shows! What does
it show?

One who has never tried it does not know that he
can double the yield of life—add immeasurably to his
understanding and his joy—by fitting words to his adventures. To live interestingly and deeply, and to tell
oneself about it afterward, is to squeeze the last drop
of nectar from the wild grapes of experience.

What freedom when a man lets himself go utterly!
That is, never stops to consider consequences, least of
all, financial consequences, before he speaks—speaks out
exactly what he is. *Is* what he is. Such and such I really
am. Take me or leave me.

Commentaries

XII

Commentaries

IF WE TAKE our friends at their best, we shall find the world full of interesting people. But we can discover their best only with our best.

This I thought, the other day, visiting the E.'s whom I have known these many years, but never before at their best, or mine.

It is certain, to an uninteresting man nothing interesting ever happens; to an interesting man, everything.

I think it no new observation, but it grows clearer in a world distraught, that men too easily cast aside one of their chief superiorities over horses, dogs, cows, geese, ducks, bees—the gift of laughter. A million years nature dripped with evolutionary sweat trying to produce a smile as a settled human achievement— and hasn't fully succeeded yet.

Panacea: in times of sadness, the strong, warm earth —the little, smiling, permanent things.

The trouble with so many men who have dollars is that they have little else.

Perfection being so far beyond my reach, I am glad enough of a little imperfection. Life on any terms is good.

"Rotten wood," remarks the old Chinaman, "cannot be carved." The true worker wants something hard to work in. Children will build with sand, but the mature man must have a granite mountain for his chisel.

When we envy another man, it is his reward that we covet, not his process; and it is only process, attitude, that brings joy. Success may or may not come to a man, and it is often ill-bestowed; but of his own attitude and process, given tranquillity, a man may be sure.

Have you found an idea robust enough to keep you away from your dinner—prevent your sleep—drive you up and down the dark country roads in the night— make you careless of cash—there must be something in such an idea.

Stop before you have said it all; be content occasionally to touch off the other fellow.

So many men attempt to explain the universe who cannot understand, much less explain, a single blade of grass.

We are constantly trying to give people good things they cannot take.

This shakes me: the poignancy of beauty seen against a background of inevitable death.

Sight may satisfy the scientist, only insight the poet.

I walked in the close, warm, semitropic night. Without darkness, man would have been vastly longer in discovering himself and his universe; without darkness, how see the stars?

Not pessimism, not optimism—equanimity!

What little nimble words it takes, words well woven and well flung, to catch the least darting insect of an idea out of the sunny air!

I have just returned from New York, and having wiped the world out of my eyes, look with joy at the earth.

A man I know likes to boast of being a "self-made man." This is well enough—if only he would finish the job.

Once I was near becoming a reformer, but through the grace of God (and my own futility) I escaped. If I had made the world, at that time, what I wanted, what a mess! Supposing I had been condemned to live in it. Since I should have had to stop growing, it would have destroyed most of the interest—and adventure—I have had since.

What irony—the Utopian condemned to live in his own Utopia! What a book! What a play! What a satire! I mean by this the Utopian who would remake the world by next Wednesday, according to a golden plan he has himself made, or adopted out of a book, not the toiling reformer who tries his remedies first on himself.

Like bees, we perish when we abandon the swarm.

All easy, quiet, natural, genuine—nothing ever put on. . . .

I had a moment this morning of sheer delight—of not feeling like doing anything, and not having anything to do.

I ran across today what I consider a perfect definition: "A seed is a young plant packed ready for transportation."

I know a man who has a sense of power only when he is buying something.

Nothing, I think, so inadequate as language: to express in words not made by oneself concepts clear only to oneself. Words worn threadbare, sizes too small! How stop a winged idea long enough to express it? Poor, inarticulate man.

Looking back, I have this to regret, that too often when I loved, I did not say so.

The price of intense living, enjoyment, is fatigue. One dies of living.

What does it matter?—I have given what I had. How give what I had not?

Nothing more withering to the soul of man than to feel himself impregnably sure, to sit in the seat of judgment, to condemn all the world that does not exactly share his views.

I know a man who regards himself always as a responsibility, a duty, a burden—never as a pleasure.

What makes a book is, of course, the author of it; what kills it also.

A mature man is one who does not have to go outside himself for his controls. A mature man is one who can trust himself with himself.

Discipline is inevitable; if it does not come from within a man, it will be imposed from without.

I go no further: I can live here.

What I have loved well, no one can ever take from me.

How nearly perfect: to know that one whom you like, likes you.

To love, begin anywhere.

It is recompense, perhaps, that people without imagination have not the imagination to know it.

Sayings to Live By

XIII

Sayings to Live By

WHEN I WAS a youngster, teaching a country school, I knew an old farmer who was a kind of walking anthology. Whenever he read anything he liked in the *Farmers' Almanac,* or the *Country Gentleman,* or *Bright Sunny Days,* a Sunday weekly he subscribed for, he used to cut it out and slip it under the sweatband of his old hat. Often I stopped to talk with him for the pure joy of seeing him, sooner or later, as he began to be excited, pull off his hat and look for the bit of verse or quotation which, as he commonly remarked, said exactly what he thought much better than he could say it himself. I remember one in particular he showed me after relating his difficulties with a neighbor who had the reputation of being cantankerous:

"Some men are like the stump the old farmer had in his field—too hard to uproot, too knotty to split, and too wet and soggy to burn. The neighbors asked him what he did about it. 'Well, now, boys,' he answered, 'if you won't tell the secret, I'll tell you. I just plowed around it.' "

I wish I could convey the delight with which my old friend read this anecdote.

"Who do you s'pose said that?" he asked. "Old Abe Lincoln said that, but by gar, I thought of it myself afore I ever knowed he said it."

Once when I turned in at his lane to visit the old farmer, he showed me longer quotations, many of them "poetry," which he had tacked upon his granary door, and even on the partitions in his horse barn. I can see him standing there, stoutly, legs apart, reading aloud some passage he delighted in.

"What do you think o' this now?" or "That's what I call sense—jes' downright sense," or "Don't that fellow know what's what!"

I thought afterward, as I tramped up the town road, how most of us have collections of sayings we live by. Most of us, in one way or another, make anthologies for ourselves. I should say that a large proportion of the sayings that country people keep or can repeat are from the Bible, or the old hymnbooks, or from Ben Franklin, or Mark Twain or Longfellow, but there are many others that are caught up out of the daily papers, waifs and strays from the magazines, bits heard over the radio, passages from the latest sermon or public address. I believe it would be difficult to find an adult human being, man or woman, who has not a saying or two, or more, that he is saving because it expresses something that is vital to him. A cynical proverb, a witty rejoinder, a bitter characterization, a smutty story, quite as much as the wisdom of the sages, releases something that the man has in him and expresses his nature.

All of these selected quotations have common characteristics: they somehow help people to go on living, or enduring, or enjoying, in an often complex or arduous or vexatious world; they all, somehow, express ideas or emotions which are dimly their own, for which they have no adequate words. In the long run, no writing survives that is not useful or helpful to some human being. Walt Whitman says somewhere in his *Democratic Vistas:*

"For a work to be esteemed good . . . it will have to satisfy the demand of all those great masses of people who are situated in the natural conditions of laborious life."

All my life I have been building up my anthology. I do not keep the quotations in the sweatband of my old hat or tack them on the doors in my barn, but the process of preserving them is much the same.

Whenever words fly up at me from the printed page, as I read, I intercept them instantly, knowing they are for me. I turn them over carefully in my mind and cling to them hard. Sometimes I commit them to memory or copy them down in my notebooks as a permanent possession, often to be taken out for my pleasure, thought about, gloated over. If men are made up largely of what they select as they go through life, as I firmly believe, these passages I have so gladly intercepted not only represent what I admire or what I like, they are in reality a part of *Me*, myself. For better or worse, for richer or poorer, for earth or for heaven, they are representative of what I am.

In this chapter, therefore, I am acting upon my own rule and setting down a few from among the hundreds of selections I have made out of many books in fifty years and more of reading. I am not saying that they are the best, since selection so often depends upon a momentary mood, but they are all passages that have at some time in my life stirred me; helped me to live and to enjoy; banished envy and anxiety, increased my courage. These are words which, as the Quakers say, have spoken to my condition. For if books do not somehow increase or liberate or amuse or fortify our lives, why go to them?

I have considered with pleasure the thought that some of these random passages may fly up out of the page to bless readers I do not know. May you love them as much as I have!

"Today I have got out of all trouble, or rather I have cast out all trouble, for it was not outside, but within. . . ."—Marcus Aurelius

"When I have attempted to join myself to others by services, it proved an intellectual trick, and no more. They eat your services like apples, and leave you out. But love them, and they feel you, and delight in you all the time."—RALPH WALDO EMERSON

I found the other day a passage in the *Specimen Days* of Walt Whitman which seems to me to go down into the depths of human experience—at least as I know it:

"After you have exhausted what there is in business, politics, conviviality, love and so on—have found that none of these finally satisfy, or permanently wear—what remains? Nature remains, to bring out from their torpid recesses the affinities of man or woman with the open air —the sun by day and the stars of the heaven by night."

"The greatest thing of the world is for a man to know how to be his owne."—MONTAIGNE, Ch. XXXVIII

I meet many men who think that peace in this world can be had as a result of a treaty, a pact, a law passed by some parliament or congress—that is, by some trick of social machinery. I think of a remark made by Woodrow Wilson during the first World War:

"The peace of the world is not going to be assured by the compact of nations, but by the sympathies of men."

Peace is inside, not outside, of human beings.

William Cobbett's first speech in Parliament began, "It appears to me, that since I have been sitting here, I have heard a great deal of vain and unprofitable conversation."

Here is an arresting line from one of Emerson's letters: "Life consists in what a man is thinking all day."

In a contemporary account of the death of Montaigne (written in 1592 or 1593) by a man who knew him, Etienne Pasquier, I find this comment:
"For the rest, do not think that his life was different from his writings."
Of all judgments none I know, I should myself more ardently prize than this.

"I am bigger than anything that can happen to me. All these things, sorrow, misfortune, and suffering, are outside my door. I am in the house, and I have the key."
This quotation from an old acquaintance of mine, Charles F. Lummis, of California, was sent me by another old friend who has had her full share of "sorrow, misfortune, and suffering." It has given her comfort.

"I cannot think Nature is so spent and decayed that she can bring forth nothing worth her former years. She is always the same, like herself; and when she collects her strength, is abler still. Men are decayed, and studies; she is not.—JONSON's *Discoveries*

[208]

This I find in my much marked copy of *Religio Medici*:

"No man can justly censure or condemn another, because indeed no man truly knows another. This I perceive in myself; for I am in the dark to all the world, and my nearest friends behold me but in a cloud. . . . Further, no man can judge another, because no man knows himself: for we censure others but as they disagree from that humour which we fancy laudable in ourselves, and commend others but for that wherein they seem to quadrate and consent with us."

"Civilization is, before all, the will to live in common. A man is uncivilized, barbarian, in the degree in which he does not take others into account."—ORTEGA, *The Revolt of the Masses*

"You shall have joy, or you shall have power," said God. "You shall not have both."—EMERSON, *Journals*

"Be not angry that you cannot make others as you wish them to be, since you cannot make yourself as you wish to be."—THOMAS À KEMPIS

Dr. Johnson must often be quoted. Here are two from Volume I of Boswell.

"No man," says he, "is obliged to do as much as he can do. A man is to have part of his life to himself."

"It is by studying little things that we attain the great

art of having as little misery and as much happiness as possible."

> *Everywhere I have sought rest*
> *And found it nowhere*
> *Save in little nooks*
> *With Books.*
>
> THOMAS À KEMPIS

> *To see the world in a grain of sand,*
> *And a heaven in a wild flower;*
> *Hold infinity in the palm of your hand,*
> *And eternity in an hour.*
>
> —WILLIAM BLAKE

"If a man does not keep pace with his companions, perhaps it is because he hears a different drummer. Let him keep step to music which he hears, however measured or far away."—HENRY D. THOREAU

"Society has, at all times, the same want, namely, of one sane man with adequate powers of expression to hold up each object of monomania in its right relations."

"True happiness," says Professor Santayana, "is once to have touched perfection . . . and not to have jogged on forever in mediocrity."

> *We die of what we eat and drink*
> *But more we die of what we think.*
> —E. A. ROBINSON, *Nicodemus*

St. Augustine says: "For the effort to make men abandon even a great evil and cleave to a great good produces more trouble than benefit, if they act merely under compulsion and not from conviction."

"The great malady of public life is cowardice. Most men are not untrue, but they are afraid. Most of the errors of public life, if my observation is to be trusted, come, not because men are morally bad, but because they are afraid of something. God knows why they should be: it is generally shadows they are afraid of."— WOODROW WILSON, Unpublished address, June 13, 1914

"I never meddle with saying what a man should doe in the world; there are over many others that doe it; but what myself doe in the world."—MONTAIGNE, Ch. XXVII

"After all, the salvation of the world depends on the men who will not take evil good-humoredly, and whose laughter destroys the fool instead of encouraging him." —BERNARD SHAW, *The Quintessence of Ibsenism*

"By all means begin your folio; even if the doctor does not give you a year, even if he hesitates about a month, make one brave push and see what can be accomplished in a week. It is not only in finished undertakings that we ought to honor useful labor. A spirit goes out from the man who means execution, which outlives the most untimely ending."—STEVENSON, *Aes Triplex*

Two from Goethe:
"To live within limits, to want one thing, or a very few things, very much and love them very dearly. Cling to them. Survey them from every angle, become one with them—that is what makes the poet, the artist, the human being."

"Agriculture is a very fine thing, because you get such an unmistakable answer as to whether you're making a fool of yourself or hitting the mark."

"A philosopher when he has all that he wants is different from a philosopher when he has not."—JOHN GALSWORTHY, *The Forsyte Saga*

Three treasures from Leonardo da Vinci:
"Whoever in discussion adduces authority uses not his intellect but his memory."

"If the thing that is loved be base, the lover becomes base."

"Intellectual passion drives out sensuality."

"Sir," said Dr. Johnson, "there is no settling the point of precedency between a louse and a flea."

So often, listening to the arguments of politicians (when I must), I recall a remark made long ago by a wise man:

"How can great minds be produced in a country," asks John Stuart Mill, "where the test of great minds is agreeing in the opinion of small minds?"

"My intelligence and heart both tell me that if it is good for me to enjoy life it is good for other people.

"I wish to order this existence, which is to me so fine and full of fun, so that I need never enjoy it at the expense of others, nor they at the expense of myself. And in the firm belief that this is a possible state of things for mankind to bring about, I go forward."—JOHN GALS-WORTHY.

Quite in line with this faith I find a sentence in Sedgwick's *Essays on Great Writers*:

"The fundamental truth of democracy is the belief that the real pleasures of life are increased by sharing them."

"Most people on this terraqueous globe eat too much, which it is, and nothing else, that makes them stupid, as also unphilosophic. To be a philosopher it is absolutely necessary to be famished. . . . Being famished, I shall show this world of ours in the next five years something that it never saw before. But if I had a regular dinner, I should sink into the general stupidity of my beloved human brethren."—DE QUINCEY, in a letter to his daughter, 1847

A word from Pantagruel:
"For all the goods that the heaven covereth, and that the earth containeth, in all their dimensions of height, depth, breadth, length, are not of so much worth, as that we should for them disturb or disorder our affections, trouble or perplex our senses or spirits."

"Better is an handful with quietness, than both the hands full with travail and vexation of spirit."

I like a great deal of Wordsworth, these lines from "Tintern Abbey," for example:

> *That blessed mood, . . .*
> *In which . . . we are laid asleep*
> *In body, and become a living soul:*
> *While with an eye made quiet by the power*
> *Of harmony, and the deep power of joy,*
> *We see into the life of things.*

I hesitate to quote Montaigne, since once I begin, he is likely to fill all my pages:
"Good Lord," he says, "how I would hate such a commendation, to be a sufficient man in writing and a foolish, shallow-headed braine or coxcombe in all things else."

[214]

"They are happy," says William Penn, in *Fruits of Solitude*, "that live retiredly. . . . They that must be enjoyed by every Body, can never enjoy themselves as they should."

This from William James, *The Will to Believe*.
"These then are my last words to you: Be not afraid of life. Believe that life *is* worth living, and your belief will help create the fact."

Today I ran across this old Greek bit (translated by J. W. Mackail) which I should like to put at the end of the last chapter of my last book:
"Dear Earth, take old Amyntichus to thy bosom, remembering his many labors on thee: for ever he planted in thee the olive-stock, and often made thee fair with vine cuttings, and filled thee full of corn, and, drawing channels of water along, made thee rich with herbs and plenteous with fruit; do thou in return lie softly over his gray temples and flower into tresses of spring herbage."

A Captivity Enriched

XIV

A Captivity Enriched

ILLNESS IS also a part of life, therefore to be well considered here. I was ill most of one bright spring. Here are the daily notes I made, just as I set them down at the time.

1. AWAITING SENTENCE

MAY 18. In the hospital. I have been here four days, most of the time in a torment of pain, now somewhat soothed and comforted. I am being prepared, a comprehensive regime of examination, rest, and medication, against the day of my ordeal—if ordeal it must be. The doctors envelop themselves in an atmosphere of mysterious, if uncommunicative, knowingness; the nurses move about in a kind of white silence, deft and gentle.

I lie here this morning propped up in my bed with the sunshine streaming in at my eastern window. I can look out into the lush spring foliage of the maple trees.

I can hear the distant, not unpleasant, sounds of the hospital. On the table are the flowers that friends have brought to me, testaments of their affection.

I had a fairly good night of it, with no pain (almost none) and no drugs, and having had my Spartan breakfast, I am full of languorous, deceptive comfort.

Every day since I have been here, oftenest at night, I have said over to myself a passage I found long ago in the book of one of the wisest of men:

"Let not future things disturb thee, for thou will come to them, if it shall be necessary, having with thee the same reason which now thou usest for present things."

I have had to plead hard for this, my notebook. Notebooks, it seems, are not to be found among the established restoratives of the materia medica; they are not mentioned in the table of contents, not set down in the index. Naturally, they do not exist. One of my doctors, however, has a kind of theoretical imagination: he knows that there is a mind as well as a brain! But even he seemed anxious to make the provision that, being granted the boon of the notebook—this comes under the precept that the sick man, within reason, must be humored—I am not to write in it. For where in the treatises on hospital practice is there any mention of the fountain pen as an instrumentality of healing? He did not know that I have been taking the fountain pen in large or small doses all my life; that I have become a hopeless addict, in danger of collapse if deprived of it. So much there is that even the experts do not know!

So, I am writing again, not under compulsion, not much at a time, certainly not for publication, but to put down the more or less vagrant comments and reflections—hardly thoughts at all—that occur to me as I lie here in captivity, awaiting final sentence. When I grow weary, or have nothing more at the moment that I want to say, I stop, even in the middle of a sentence, and put my notebook away in the little drawer near the head of my bed. This drawer, not a foot square, easily holds every personal possession I now need or can use.

After the first day or so, should not a man be able to use his illness? If he cannot do his usual work, enjoy his usual excursions, his friends, his food—even his sleep—is there not still a margin of life wherein he can dwell happily? There are books, so long as he can read them; there are friends who come in; there are strange new people that pass by in the corridor or come in at the door. If one could see keenly and deeply enough, he should not need more than a window-square of life to know a continent. Above all, a man has the rich country of his own mind to travel in. Released from absorbing daily occupations, he finds his thoughts going out in all directions, considering events, considering his friends and his own strange life, considering books he has read or intends to read—all with a new and calm perspective. This is something! The days may still be precious. If he have the secret of enjoyment, a little forced idleness, even pain—even a good deal of pain— should not devour him.

MAY 19. So many things that happen in a hospital I did not anticipate; and some that I anticipated, some of the worst, have not happened at all—as yet. I have renewed my ancient acquaintance with the sunrise, which I do not remember to have seen before in years. The sun came up this morning about half past five. I saw it first just above the sill at the lower left-hand corner of my window. It was already above the lilac bush, near the edge of the wall. It bloomed in glory and began at once to curve upward at quite an unex-pected angle across the glass. As I lay watching, it touched and obliterated the window cord; it was mo-mentarily dimmed by the wooden muntin, it crossed two telephone wires, and then presently, scarce an hour from its rising, it set in glory behind the lower edge of the window shade. . . .

This enjoyable discovery I did not anticipate; neither did I anticipate, truth to tell, the weary long hours before even the nurse appeared; longer still before my breakfast was brought in.

I am in pain again; but no matter how miserable in body, or low in mind, if I can write even a few lines, I immediately feel better.

I remembered this morning that W. H. Hudson wrote one of his best books, *Far Away and Long Ago,* while ill in bed. Stevenson wrote in bed. Mark Twain wrote in bed. Goethe wrote in bed. And I have little doubt that, if we could know, Shakespeare wrote in bed—although I never found a line in his plays to prove it.

What a tragedy—life deferred, not lived. Life feared, doubted, rejected, not gloriously accepted. Did you think you could have the good without the evil; joy without sorrow; rest without labor?

MAY 20. I have had a reasonably quiet day, not without pain, nevertheless bearable, and improving with the passage of the hours. The doctors are still uncommunicative, and I ask no questions. Having accepted the authority of the surgeon, I am resting upon it. When a man has invoked the best available knowledge and skill he can find, nothing that he can do or say or think can change anything. I do not, therefore, worry.

Nothing lasts—not even pain: this thought is comforting.

When life circumscribes and establishes painful new limitations, may it not drive us down into the deeper springs of understanding? Not being able to go abroad, may we not go deep? Go high?

"Warmth, food, sleep, and a book," said Hazlitt. Blissful fundamentals—if a man is not in pain.

Of friends who come to a hospital, so few are themselves. Often they seem like embarrassed strangers with whom one must become acquainted all over again. A husk to be broken, a constraint to be eased!—and so little strength for doing either. Often there is pity, which one does not want; not humor, which one does. Blustering, unnatural heartiness to cheer the poor invalid and, still worse, corroborative narratives showing how much greater misery the visitor has suffered. See what I am now!

Best of all in a visitor, I think, is the rare gift of quiet commonplace, oblivious to the embarrassment of the moment, lifting one out of the atmosphere of the sick room into the normal things of the pleasant world outside. It is not the exceptional or the extreme that a sick man wants; he has that already and is weary of it; he longs for unthinking normality. And, if it may be—but that is asking for the miraculous—the goodly quiet gift of laughter in which he may genuinely join.

MAY 21. Wonder of wonders! I am to be allowed a BOOK.

A CAPTIVITY ENRICHED

"In a day or two, if he keeps on feeling better," said the doctor, speaking across my bed to the immaculate nurse, "he may have a book." It is a way doctors have: talking over you, not to you, and thus stilling any rebelliousness that may be arising within you and at the same time commenting hopefully upon your progress.

A book! What book? I feel like the boy in the old fairy tale—offered a single wish. What if I should make a mistake? This requires thought. Of all the millions of books in the libraries and bookshops of America, what *one* shall I choose? I know a million or two offhand that I *don't* want.

I have been going through a round of treatments, not so much painful as disagreeable. I suppose there is not more of the disagreeable in a hospital than there is outside, but it is more concentrated, and one has less vitality for meeting it. The place of the disagreeable in human life, and how human beings react to it: an entire philosophy could be built upon these considerations; and a system of ethics upon the mechanism of avoidance and transmutation. . . .

I am certainly easier as to the pain, but weary. I do not even feel like writing.

Anything understood is beautiful—but there is no art without the artist.

A horse's hoofs on the pavement in the early morning sound, at a distance, exactly like the stropping of a razor.

MAY 22. I am sitting on the broad sunny east porch of the hospital, where I can look off into the lush spring foliage of maples and basswood and tulip trees. Near at hand a clump of bush honeysuckles fills all the air with fragrance, and I can see at greater distance a large horse-chestnut tree in full bloom. A mother robin on the lawn is feeding her family of young, grown now to be as large as she. A pair of pigeons on the roof edge are making ardent love; and all about lies a world of infinite beauty and peace.

I had a hard day of it yesterday and last night, with hours of pain which seemed at times utterly unbearable. This morning I am in that mood of weary languor when the body, so recently in torment, is momentarily at rest. This week my preparation should certainly be put to the test. Anything should be better than this; anything that would stop this pain.

It was a delight to have several friends come in; one of them, and the dearest, came with daffodils. . . .

I wonder, did you really expect to escape the common ills of mankind? Did you expect to choose the ill that best suited you, caused you the least pain?

Primary things—primary things—not yet learned. . . .

A CAPTIVITY ENRICHED

In love, could anything be worse than paleness?
Dimness? To take hold of life loosely, weakly, vaguely?

MAY 23. I have had a delightful experience this morning—to me, here in captivity, one singularly moving.

"Quick, Miss Manning," said I, "throw up the window!"

Where I lie propped up, I can just see a little
meadow, all green with new grass and whitened here
and there with the ripened seed balloons of the dan-
delion. As I looked out this morning, I caught a flash
of wings, then another and another. I thought at first
it was a blackbird, but there was something alluringly
different, suggesting a quite unbelievable possibility.

"Quick, Miss Manning," said I, "throw up the window."

With clearer vision I knew instantly what it was. A
bobolink! Here, in this bit of meadow in the midst of
the noisy town, a bobolink lifting, poising, fluttering—
no doubt singing its immortal song, only I could not
hear it for the roar of the distant street and the incessant inner hum of the hospital corridor. There he was,
just as I have so often watched him, lifting and singing,
just such May weather, so many, many years, in my
own meadow.

I cannot possibly express the lift and the thrill the
vision gave me; the sense, here in my weakness, of
something in nature immeasurably dependable. Some-

thing inexhaustible, that one sore-pressed could rest back upon and be at peace. I think I never in all my life before had such a sense of the imperturbability, the continuity, of nature. Every May the same sweetness and serenity of beauty; every spring these millions of years. I felt my whole soul swelling with love of it. Storms, yes; the rage of the frost and the snow; insect hordes; blights; rusts; diseases; the implacable law of the jungle—and yet this morning in May, here in this calm meadow, the bobolink lifting and singing! What courage, what endurance, what beauty—and what serenity. For a blinding moment it seemed to me that the only refuge, the only security left for the torn spirit of man was in nature—the love of nature, the study of nature; that humble effort to understand, which is science; that imaginative interpretation, which is art.

Something all day has been ringing little bells of joy in my heart.

MAY 24. This is the tenth day of my captivity. I can see that I am not satisfying the doctors. I am not doing as well as they hoped. It is not in what they say; it is in what they do not say.

I know it myself: I do not need anyone, doctor or nurse, to tell me. I have been in pain again, nearly the worst I have had.

He who has learned how to live, I think, has learned how to die.

The inconceivable sum of human suffering! I have known of it long as a *fact*, never before as an *experience;* and there is all the difference in the world between the two. Diabolical human torture here in this hospital, known and seen and heard. Skill and sympathy help allay it, but there it is, the grim primeval terror, as unappeasable as it is inevitable. Not death; death is kind. Death has mercy. But tortured bodies and reeling minds! There will come a time—I shall not live to see it—when human sympathy and human sense will have reached the point where it will not be the supreme effort of science, exercising every ingenuity, to prolong the anguish in wracked human frames where any semblance of normal life has disappeared and where death would be the supreme blessing. They know, they know, these skillful men! And society could well entrust such a decision, not perhaps to any one physician, but certainly to a properly constituted body of medical judges, whose gift of death would be an incalculable blessing, not only to the sufferer, but to all his friends. That time will come.

Above everything, beyond everything, to face the *reality* and not to give way! Wherever we go, we human beings, we must take our pain with us. It is as much the stuff of our life as joy; and he who thinks that he can live without dealing with it, one way or another, is a fool. What pathetic dependence upon pseudo science! What miracles! What magic! And did you think that

Life would not finally face you down? That Reality would not look you in the eye? In the corner there where you cower, in the midst of your mumbled incantations, Life will get you at last. You have drugged yourself? There will be pain that no drug can deaden. Will you cower there like a lashed slave until death mercifully relieves you?

Or will you refuse, utterly and irretrievably, to be fooled into the belief that there is any way finally, by any magic whatsoever, be it religious or scientific, to dodge Reality? That there is any way out becoming to a man except to face Life honestly and fearlessly?

Slavery to fear comprises the whole life of a multitude of men. Almost every pure joy of life comes of the effort to look at life clearly, honestly, understandingly; to know its realities. To face it; to meet its grimmest challenges. There art has its roots; there the passion to see, which is science, has its deep beginnings. Everything that is creative arises out of the effort to know the truth, and knowing it, to use it. And it is only where there is fearless honesty that there can be joy.

So now, be still!

May 25. Eleventh day. I am somewhat easier but at the price of utter weariness—I do not even want the book I was promised the other day.

Other men have passed this way; other men have had this experience, and for long afterward have lived their lives. I may yet be free again. . . .

Several visitors today. The doctors frown on them: I enjoy them—J. with white iris. . . .

Montaigne (I think) somewhere says: "God has given me winter according to my wool, and suffering according to my power of withstanding it." This is a comforting thought. Every man, certainly, has a *little* less trouble than he can bear.

When men are in hospital "johnnies," all human distinctions are set aside. The democracy of illness!

MAY 26. Twelfth day. Rolling dark clouds and rain: a morning of somber silence; but by ten o'clock the sun was up and out, and nature began again to smile. I have been much alone all day.

I write a little here, a few lines, a few words, and rest down among my pillows, rising again soon to write a little, a few lines, a few words. . . .

I have been almost comfortable today, and therefore almost hopeful. The nights are the worst.

What do men do who have nothing within when life stops them? How endure the misery of vacuity in

addition to physical pain? Or am I wrong: is vacuity a
blessing in a time like this?

Curious the things that come into one's mind—this
remark of Thoreau after the hanging of John Brown:

"I meet him at every turn. He is more alive than
ever he was."

The other day, this quotation came in without
knocking:

> *God guard me from the thoughts men think*
> *In the mind alone;*
> *He who sings a lasting song,*
> *Thinks in his marrow-bone.*

On a day like this, with spring in the world, I want
most of all to escape—at any cost to get away anywhere
from this captivity. The other day, when most in pain,
I was all for fighting! Today my courage oozes out at
my finger tips: I'd run if I could. The bars are too
strong, the watchers too alert—and I am boundlessly
weak. I suppose a man is not more in captivity here
than he is there—inside as outside—but what he has
there is his own strength—and his faith in it.

One thing that a man keeps, if he keeps anything,
and that is his imagination, his waking dreams; and
sometimes, even in pain and weariness, they comfort
him.

When I am propped up in my bed, I can look out across a little field, a lane, a hedgerow of trees, to the distant country road. At first it interested and amused me. I counted the cars going by during specimen quarter hours, morning, noon, and night—and tried to reason why more came out in the evening, when men should be going home, than went in during the morning. I counted the trucks separately, and the busses, and the red cars and yellow cars, and reckoned the percentages. I even tried to time various vehicles from the moment I first saw them rounding the little bend in the road until they disappeared behind my window frame. By such trivial diversions a man may wear away the dull hours of his captivity.

Quite suddenly, the other afternoon, I grew weary of the road; I shut my eyes; I wanted no more of it. Such tireless motion fatigued and irritated me. So many human beings coming and going upon errands I could not know, to places I could not guess. It was a free world and beautiful—and I had no part in it.

This distaste lasted some time, but this morning, when the traffic was at its height, and most exciting— quite without premeditation, but with the lift that welcomes a daring idea—I stopped one of those cars and got in.

It was a fine, great car, westward bound, and I traveled along with it to Florence and Leeds and Hayden-ville. I looked out at the old mills by the river, the church on the sunny square, and the pleasant hills beyond. And so, presently, I reached Williamsburg, the waysides all glorious with May morning; every house I passed seemed hospitable to me, and every man I met seemed happy; and so I came at length to Goshen, on the mountaintop. I saw the wide fields and old stone fences smothered in cherry bloom; and the noble great pines I saw, marching like grenadiers along every hillside. I saw the Inn. I saw the Congregational church, all in white, pointing its finger heavenward.

I have been familiar for many years with every turn and dip of these country roads. "But I think," said I, "that I never knew the country more beautiful than it is today." "I do not remember," I said, "of ever enjoying a trip more than I do this." For I saw everything not merely with the well-remembering eye, embossed with the lichens of memory—visits I had made alone, and visits with well-loved friends—but with a strange new ardency of escape that I never felt before. I recalled the discussions I had with a friend of mine when we drove these roads, always in apple-blossom time, to fish for trout in Barrus Brook. I took my lordly time, for time I had in plenty, to stop often and look long and think deep, before I returned here safely to my bed and rested back among my pillows.

I cannot tell what joy I have been having of these unpremeditated travels, how I can thus forget myself into felicity awhile. I shall go again, I shall be bolder in stopping swift cars by the wayside and taking passage in them to the dear familiar places among the hills of Goshen—perhaps far beyond the hills of Goshen. . . .

This day, at least, has not been wholly lost.

2. PAIN

MAY 27. Thirteenth day. The nights are the worst: the nights when one is most alone; when one needs most to rest. I thought yesterday I was really getting better: I was mistaken. The pain last night was the worst I have had—if that were possible. The doctors and nurses have apparently done the best they could, short of complete anesthesia—and accomplished exactly nothing.

Last night I had recourse again to the little red-bound book which has given me such comfort through the years. No such discipline in fortitude have I anywhere found as in this precious book. Several passages I have long known by heart, but it always helps to look them up where in past times I have scored the pages, and read them aloud, or repeat them just under my breath.

"In every pain let this thought be present, that there is no dishonor in it, nor does it make the governing intelligence worse. Indeed, in the case of most pains, let this remark of Epicurus aid thee, that pain is neither intolerable nor everlasting, if thou bearest in mind that it has its limits, and if thou addest nothing to it in imagination. . . . (by which he means worry).

"Pain is either an evil to the body—then let the body say what it thinks of it—or to the soul; but it is in the power of the soul to maintain its own serenity and tranquillity, and not to think that pain is an evil."

But the whole doctrine of Marcus Aurelius relating to pain is in a line that does not refer directly to pain at all: "Nothing happens to any man which he is not formed by nature to bear."

How ridiculous, to think that the little white crystals of the physician can physic pain. I have had them, I know! A moment of blessed surcease, perhaps, and there again is old Truepenny, deep in the cellarage: "What now, old mole, canst travel so fast!" The physician with his phials and his needles can indeed rob us of our consciousness—but that is death. If we live, sooner or later, regardless of the wit of man, we have pain to face: a reality; a final unescapable, immutable fact of life. What poor souls, if we have then no philosophy to face it with.

A mechanism of delay in meeting the ultimate realities of life; that is all that science, after stupendous toil, has been able to produce. And we, poor creatures, inventing, discovering, building with ever increasing energy, think we are finding a cure! We think we have found, or are finding, some mechanism outside ourselves which will take the place of the courageous and enduring human soul.

Late afternoon. I am easier again; at the moment I feel no pain at all. I fell into an exhausted sleep after my luncheon and awakened feeling much rested and comforted. The doctor was in to reassure me. Mine is an up-and-down illness, with excursions and alarms. I am almost encouraged.

To add to my other reassurances, I now have the BOOK promised to me. I have several books. They are arranged here on my table, where I can see the backs of them, as in my own library.

"Here is your book," said the cheerful nurse the other morning, when I was resting on the sunny porch.

The nurse had given me my morning medicine, she had plumped out my pillows and patted down my coverlet—she is a genius at bedmaking—and she was now eying me approvingly.

"Here, now," said she, "is your book."

I was much surprised.

"What is it?" I asked.

"Oh," said she, "it's a—— I got it at the hospital library."

"Oh," said I.

It was indeed a book. It had been prescribed, and

she had now administered it. I had never heard of the book the nurse had brought me, nor the author of it. I held it in my hands. A book, any book, might prove curative.

At the same time, I reflected with some amusement upon all the thought I had given to what book I should read when I had won the rare privilege of reading anything at all. What book to read at this moment of my life, under these peculiar conditions! I had moments of feeling like some Robinson Crusoe cast away on a desert isle. What book would he choose? Fiction or non-fiction, biography or autobiography (which I have always liked well), Charles Lamb's *Letters*, the writings of the old philosophers, Boswell's *Johnson* (a good book to last a long time), or Mark Twain perhaps? I thought of books dealing with the sorry problems of a torn world, and promptly dismissed them, being sufficiently torn in my own right. Old books or new books? Inspirational books? *Pickwick Papers*? Books for sheer enjoyment?

"Do you think," I said to the nurse, "you could get me a copy of *Pride and Prejudice*, by Jane Austen?"

My request greatly surprised me: it came out so promptly and unexpectedly. I had not thought especially of Jane Austen; I had not read *Pride and Prejudice* for many years. But there it was decided! Why not reread Jane Austen?

The nurse was gone a long time. She could not find *Pride and Prejudice*.

"There's a book in the library," she volunteered hesitatingly, "called, *The Pride of Oriskany.*"

"That," said I, "must be a different kind of pride."

"Oh," said the nurse.

J. was shocked, when she came in, to find that I could not get the book I wanted and soon brought me my own copies of *Pride and Prejudice* and *Mansfield Park*—and various other books she knew that I liked already, and others, new books, she thought I might wish to see.

After J. had gone, I opened one of the new books at random. I don't usually expect much of new books, but there, at the very page I opened it, I found a nugget of a quotation worth thinking about. It was a definition of civilization by Lord Russell of Killowen:

"Its true signs are thought for the poor and suffering, chivalrous regard and respect for women, the frank recognition of human brotherhood, irrespective of race or color or nation or religion, the narrowing of the domain of force as a governing factor in the world, the love of ordered freedom, abhorrence of what is mean and cruel and vile, ceaseless devotion to the claims of justice."

MAY 28. Fourteenth day. Boisterous clouds and a cool, sharp wind. This day I am content; the doctor has been in and passed final sentence. It is to be next Monday forenoon. J. does my dreading for me, which is unfortunate, since it need not be done at all. Why suffer twice for an ill?

This has been a day memorable for nothing but dull endurance. The pain has not been as severe as it was, but continuous, gnawing, almost as irritating as if it were sharp.

There is a stage of culture that is satisfied with names. Having named a bird, a shell, a star, a man, an institution, a disease—its creative curiosity is appeased. Each fact, after desiccation, is plainly ticketed and put away in its own little dusty pigeonhole: and Culture charges on to the capture of new facts, the ruthless determination of new names.

When a man discovers that creative knowledge does not end with names, but begins with them, he is learning to think.

MAY 29. Fifteenth day. Goethe said of an illness "attended with terrible pains": "I have learned much in illness which I could have learned nowhere else in life." This is true. He said in the same connection: "Misfortune is also a good." This I find in Lewes' *Life* (page 61) which I am rereading for the third time.

I have been thinking much about pain. How could I help it? I couldn't get away from it! I have certainly been easier, much easier, during the last few days, even though I did have one sharp attack during last night.

I had never thought of it before, but there must be an inner as well as an outer technique for meeting pain, based on the power of the soul to maintain its own serenity.

When I first came in here, I had several attacks which I thought I could not bear. I tried grim opposition: obstinate and unthinking endurance: set teeth, muscles rigid, breath hard-held. I knew that it could not last; nothing in such extreme ever lasts. Thus I bore the fiery cycle of the paroxysms, taking some credit to myself for the obstinacy of what I considered courage, but which was really fear. I do not know how it may be in other cases—for pain is as various as life itself—but I began to reflect that if these seizures were inevitable, all the force of my opposition, the sweat on my face, was a useless waste of strength and in the end, since failure was certain, a weakening of morale. "That pain which lasts a long time is tolerable." And suddenly it came to me, as a kind of new light, that I would no longer resist and struggle; I would accept the unavoidable. If it was in the nature of my disease, what else that was wise could I do? And so, each time as the paroxysm approached, I began to let go. I began to accept. I began to relax. At first the torment, ravaging unrestrained, seemed even worse than before. It consumed me utterly. But I had a glimmering sense that I was at least playing a voluntary part in my own destiny; that, somehow, I was substituting reason for blind, involuntary, fear-driven resistance. This effort I continued through the greater part of one terrible night, failing often, unable to yield completely, driven by red-hot scourges into the old resistances. At dawn, in spite of the best medication the doctors knew, I was exhausted, but I began to feel that I was on the way toward what might be, for me, a new method.

This I practiced faithfully and with increasing confidence for some time. I no longer resisted the inevitable! I am not sure that there was a great decrease in the actual physical suffering; I do know that the period of the paroxysm was reduced, since resistance seemed merely to prolong it. But the great reward was in the *mind:* in my own ability to command myself in the face of such a catastrophe; to preserve my equanimity; to rest securely upon reason when panic might so easily overwhelm me. I had moments in the midst of such paroxysms during the earlier nights when I was so secure in mind, so tranquil, that I felt it did not much matter what happened to my body. *Nothing could touch me.*

I even wondered if there was not some such easing technique for meeting death? I wondered if what happened to the body in that last stern paroxysm was not equally inconsequential?

But I was too sure of myself: I was too certain I had learned the "technique of endurance."

To talk of pain is like talking of life, so various is it. The cunning old devil! What tricks he knows. He was here long ages before I was born; and will be here—what a time!—after I have gone away. Well he knows when his victims, lulled by watching and weariness into rest, are weakest. *He* never sleeps; day nor night, *he* never rests.

All that I have said about my earlier experiences is true enough. I did learn how in part to circumvent him, *one* way I learned, but it was by the precious process of giving him all the field—of stepping aside and refusing to fight in such a sordid battle. Let him ravage, let him do his worst, he could not touch me where my life really was! Well, it seemed a grand thing to do, to be able to do, and it gave me vast comfort—a kind of tranquillity, or conceit, to the spirit. It made the man master in his own house, or made him *think* he was, which momentarily amounts to the same thing. Philosophies have been based upon this idea, and religions upon the practice of it.

But it rests upon the assumption that body and spirit can really be separated: that one can, by fiat, take command and wholly dominate the other. For moments or days, perhaps even for years, this may be true; but the old demon is only lying in wait. This little insect of a human being, thinking he is God! Thinking that life is two and not one! Thinking he can dismiss *me!* I will brew me now new poisons. I will heat me now new irons, sharpen me new pincers. I will teach him at length the lesson it is hardest of all for him to learn.

I had tried the Grand Manner, and it comforted the soul of me. It may be well to practice if one can; it is something, at the end of the fable, to go out the Hero.

But in the night—in the long night, here in the hospital bed, when I was already weary with the struggle, when all my forces were low and the spirit dim, Pain suddenly rushed my defenses, broke through my well-built walls. I had no time to gather my spirit in tranquillity. I could not accept the inevitable. I could not stand aside and see my land laid waste. I was taken by surprise; I did not know this ruse, nor the cruelty of it. I was panic-stricken. I was lost; I let everything go. I am ashamed, but it is the truth, I beat my head, I tore at my hair, I bit my wrist. I groaned and gasped. All my high thoughts trailed in the dust of my retreat.

Gradually, as this was repeated through one terrible night, I saw the childishness of it. It was utterly without reason. I saw that. What good did it do to cry out and beat one's head and bite one's flesh? Did it decrease by a single jot the torment of the pain? And did it not break down the fastnesses of the mind? Did it not destroy the man in me? I began, therefore, haltingly at first, to try another method. Instead of crying out, bemoaning myself, I said when the pain came on: "I can bear this. It is bitter, but I have known worse. I can be still, and endure it." Or I said, "This pain will

not last: it never has lasted. I shall soon be at peace."
This last, since it seemed so beautiful to me, I repeated
again and again. "I shall soon be at peace." This seemed
at the time a great improvement, as indeed I think it
really was. It did not deny the pain; it did not step aside
and give it the battlefield; it accepted it as a reality; it
declared the intention of the sovereign soul, if it could
not master it, to endure it. This was more than mere
endurance: it was hope. It was predicated—I see
now how soundly—upon one of the few human certainties: that no matter what a condition may be, it
will change. *It will change*. And so I could say to myself, "I shall soon be comfortable again; I shall be at
peace." For I knew well, deep down, that *if* I could endure, I should be better. I should know greater ease. If
I could *not* endure, it was equally plain that I should
still have peace—permanent, enduring, unawakening,
wholly painless peace. I cannot tell with what vivid as-
surance, like the word of God, these thoughts came to
me in my agony—to guide me and keep me. It seemed,
in one blind, anguished moment, that I knew better
than ever before the meaning of life and, indeed, how
to live it.

But I must, in all honesty, make a further confession.
Even though I had come into this wisdom, as it seemed
clearly to me to be, I found myself too weak—again and
again too weak—to practice it wholly. I would begin
with the words that invoked endurance; I would dwell

upon the certainty of my hope, that I could bear the pain, that it could not last, that when it was over I should know comfort, I should be at peace—the very word peace became as beautiful to me as the sunrise this morning in May—and then, under the fury of the attack, my defenses would give way, and I would slip back into misery. And yet I have gained something. I have gained much: I know what to do even if I cannot practice it fully or always successfully.

This is as far as I can now see: I can see no further.

MAY 30. Sixteenth day. "We all love to instruct," says Jane Austen, in *Pride and Prejudice*, "though we can teach only what is not worth knowing."

What fresh joy have I been having from the rereading of *Pride and Prejudice!* There are lines and paragraphs and pages in Jane Austen which seem to me to equal, if not excel, any in all English literature (that I know) in delivering to the reader with a kind of magical clairvoyance the very essence of a person or an event. These are not mere words: they are life itself. For they make the same indelible impression upon the mind and never again forsake the memory.

I did not remember the power and the genius of Jane Austen. There are passages of Shakespearean magic; the wit of another Sheridan! I have also been rereading *Barchester Towers:* but how pedestrian Anthony Trollope compared with this vivid lady.

[246]

I have been relatively easy all day—not only with a free body, but a clearer mind. I know well it is transitory: I think of next Monday. But it is glorious to have even this respite.

Having written, I lie back quietly to meditate; having meditated, I rise up again to write.

Two Rules:
Act always as though you were going to live forever.
Act always as though you were going to die on Monday.

To know what at any given time is inevitable and what is not—is not that one of the chief attainments of wisdom? In the dim zone where inevitability leaves off and controllability begins, civilization has its roots and finds its congenial climate. Here science originates, and thought wins its greatest triumphs; here ethics plants its true foundations, and statesmanship rears upon them the noblest of its compromises. Here one finds the fertile soil wherein will germinate, and, if cultivated, grow into beauty, the oak of one's own character. For it is in clear differentiation that wisdom most delights.

A wise man can live well at any time, in any place, in any society. . . .

MAY 31. Sunday. Seventeenth day. The best yet. It is proof of the doctor's regimen and medication that I am

feeling, so far as my general health is concerned, re-
markably vigorous, deceptively well. I am approaching
the ordeal of tomorrow (I am told) in the best possible
condition. The day itself is warm and still and sunny.
I have been sitting out. J. came at four, bringing as fine
a bouquet of iris as ever I saw in my life. They glorify
the room.

How a man has come to be what he is—that is the
one work of art inherent in every life—if it could but
be written with luminous understanding. *Every life!*
For no matter how low, or sad, or evil, it is a strange thing
and a marvelous that any man should be alive in this
world, that he should have a history, possibly a purpose,
even though he himself may be ignorant of either. How
did he come to be *here;* how at *this* time? What does he
mean; what does he *mean,* if anything, to himself, and
what to his family, his town, his nation, his generation?
If by rare chance, one in a million, he should not only
be acted upon, but with some gleam of self-knowledge,
some power of self-direction—some blessed gift of vision
—he should think and act upon his own power as a free
spirit—what a noble work of art is this, how fascinating,
how beautiful!

"Think only of the past," says Jane Austen, in *Pride
and Prejudice,* "as its remembrance gives you pleasure."
I am thus fortified in thinking of the past sixteen
days I have been here in this hospital. When all is said

and whatever happens on Monday, I have enjoyed this strange experience. In spite of periods of tormenting pain, and much weakness and weariness, I have not for a long time, it seems to me, known a clearer mind, nor felt such a capacity for curiosity and exploration. It may be due in part to an attention relaxed, a mind set free, from the domineering concentration of my life for months—yes, years—past. The responsibilities, the duties, the difficulties, the daily tale of bricks without straw— all cast aside!

No voluntary relinquishment of my work would ever have yielded the same sense of liberation. Elbow-nudging duty would have urged the unflagging prosecution of a task already too much delayed. I should be thinking of obligations demanding satisfaction, and loyalties requiring continued proof of their validity. But with volition taken wholly out of a man's hands, and the body set aside in regimented confinement—the leisure and the peace of a little room—how the spirit takes wings unto itself, goes vagabonding in sunny weather. How fresh and sweet the morning atmosphere of the mind! To be free to do absolutely what it will. To rest, to read, to think, to rest again—to watch a window-sized world drift by upon its insubstantial errands, to talk or not to talk with the strange, different, interesting people who come and go, seeking glimpses into their curious lives— and thus to rest again and think and read and write. And write! And read! And think!

This may truly be a captivity, as I have been thinking of it, with escape as the dearest possibility. But I wonder! Captivity for captivity, is this more grievous than that of the world outside?

Suffering, yes, if it pays the price; but does it pay the price? How much there is to buy; how costly!

3. ORDEAL

JUNE 1. Eighteenth day. A fine, warm spring morning. I am to celebrate, assisted by three doctors and numerous nurses, at noon today. I am feeling pretty well, due in part probably to the medication I have already had.

I have a few hours yet. I am going to think and write of the pleasantest experiences I have had in this hospital since I came here.

So many of the finest adventures of my life have come out of the discovery of strange new human beings, making new friendships, arriving at new acceptances and understandings.

Much as I love the printed page, I would rather be a reader of life than of books. With what enjoyment I practice the cunning art of inciting that appetite for autobiography that exists in every human being. How I enjoy leading my victims along, a little tremulously and suspiciously at first, until they reach the point where, casting all fear aside, they plunge off the deep end of fact into the refreshing ocean of their hopes, their illusions, their fears. I love to see them create, out of the drab colors of their daily lives, the roseate vision of what they think they are, cleverly fabricated out of the tenuous ideals, as iridescent as star dust, of what they would like to be. Every man has many autobiographies. I think I get the best of them.

What strange and interesting people have I met even within the confines of this little world!

I have had a-going half a dozen delightful autobiographies, each cut up into short installments—a few moments while my dinner is being brought, or my back rubbed, or at night when I am taking my medicine—the momentary pause after the consultation, the leisurely conversation with friends who come in—each brief, each soon to be continued. Nor are they like stories too easily read from the dull pages of a book, for one gets out of them in narrative only what he puts into them in sly questions, teasing innuendo, statements that positively must be refuted, bits of philosophy agreed to or disputed; and finally, the rock of personality, or at least the bump of self-esteem, having been struck with the magic rod, how delightful to watch the fountain of confidences burst forth! And autobiography so soon and so easily expands into biography, for in a small community where there have been years of association, what autobiography is reluctant to disclose, biography stands by, slyly ready to complete.

It is a sport not unlike fishing for trout, a hundred
casts without so much as a strike, a thousand to land a
little one—but once, in some still pool at the turn of a
long afternoon, when hope is beginning to dissolve in
weariness, and one is beginning to doubt even his best
fly, the big one strikes. The big one strikes, and the day
is an epoch, and the place never again to be forgotten. . . .

So many pretty little stories have I heard—a glistening
little new ring shown to me—so many comic interludes,
and episodes of sadness and suffering which even professional commonplace cannot rob of all their poignancy.

And thus, at length, slowly unfolding, the full-length
human comedy I have been eagerly casting for, yet
scarcely expected to land. It has been developing ever
since I have been here, the characters one after another
stepping into the scene and beginning—what could be
more thrilling—to move, speak, live! Time making room
for itself, reaching backward through the months and
the years; each episode more firmly establishing itself,
the details pricked in with remembered emotion. Incidents of busy streets and shaded lanes—a wholly new
geography! And then, finally, the grand moment. I
knew it might be expected—when the keynote of the
entire story—the core, the plot—came out.

It is, I can see, great enough, universal enough—this story—to be lived with, lived into, *realized,* and told finally, if one had but the time, in a full-length novel full of deep, strange, compelling passions of the human heart. I could hardly sleep the other night for thinking of it. A still greater wonder remains: the story is at this moment alive, unfinished; the characters in it are living people, at this moment moving in common streets, speaking casually in chance meeting places. A few weeks ago there was a death among them; a few weeks hence there is to be a marriage. It was out of these commonplace facts, the chance mention of them, that my story has grown.

What a thing is this: that I can lie here in this little room playing with all these new people, hearing them speak, act—represent themselves and explain themselves, all at my command—and at the same time I can watch the story, out there in real life, march onward to new adventures wherein, I can see, there will be all the old problems of temperament, character, and iron circumstance. They think with this happy marriage so near at hand that there is to be a new song upon the earth, a new Jerusalem, with angels twanging their harps—but *we* know, *we* know. Have we not seen the past? Could we not tell them what to do? How to continue happy? We know! We could! Would they listen? They would not. But their past, if momentarily forgotten, is creeping stealthily after them, as relentless as their own shadows—most relentless of all when the sun is shining most brightly. . . .

I have just been interrupted.

"The doctor is coming in," said my nurse with the faintest touch of controlled excitement in her voice.

I know what it means: I must put aside my pen. . . .

June 2. Nineteenth day. Less than the dust!

June 3. Twentieth day. Miserable day: much pain.

June 4. Twenty-first day. Cooler after intense heat. I am easier, but weak, weak. Weakness is even worse than pain.

June 5. Twenty-second day. Low barometer, but I think gradually rising. Vast relief to the mind, at least. J. has been coming faithfully every afternoon at four, and today one or two other friends. I have managed to write *something* every day, if only a few words.

In illness, things in which one thinks himself indispensable somehow get themselves serenely accomplished. No one is indispensable: even the greatest presidents, statesmen, leaders—even prophets, saints, and poets—are speedily replaced, and life goes on.

June 6. Twenty-third day. Much better, but still close in bed. I would not have believed that one good long night of painless sleep—the first in many weeks—would have wrought such a miracle of restoration. I am extremely weak, but comfortable. The doctor, however, is cautious as to the future.

I am able to read again—and write, a little at a time.

Defer life—and lose it. Wrestle with *this* moment; do not let it go until it blesses you.

Almost everything I see I am interested in; almost everyone I meet I like. . . .

We circulate not by what we write—though clever writing may arouse a transient interest—but by what we are.

The arrogance—the temerity—after all, the futility—of those who would regulate the world and do not yet know themselves, much less regulate themselves.

I like people and seem unable to do anything about it! When I entered the hospital, there was *one* person that I knew on sight I should detest. I was in that mood anyway: I was irritated, I was in pain, and above all, I did not relish the experience I was facing. I did not like the *look* of him, nor the tone of his voice. In an instant of time I had decided, in my mind, the quality of his

[255]

antecedents, and knew well all the reasons why I could not endure him. The next time I saw him I detested him still more, and was appalled to find that, in spite of everything, it was necessary for me to have more or less intimate contact with him. This led, although I resisted the impulse, to conversation—it couldn't be helped—and I soon began to find out about his family, his parents, where he came from, why and how he had come to be here, what he had done in the past, the things he liked best—as newspapers (he never read a book in his life), moving pictures, music, kinds of automobiles, and a hundred and one other things. During our conversations, his whole life began to come out, like a photographic plate in the developing fluid. I could see all the virtues he had—and they were not few—as well as all his limitations—for his smallnesses were worse than his vices. I could even follow the flight of his roving dreams.

Presently I began to like to see the man come in. I couldn't help it, for I was always thinking, while he was away, of circumstances regarding him that I did not fully understand. It was a joy to me, by leading the conversation, to explore all the shadowy spots; it was like a continued story that daily came alive to my questioning.

The more I understood of his life and of how, within the circle of his powers, he had used it, the more I came to sympathize with him; in short, I began to like him. He is not highly intelligent, he has little learning, and he has in the course of his life made many mistakes, one or two bad ones, but he seems to have used his powers, *under the circumstances,* singularly well. He has made more of himself than one might have expected. Many an abler man I know I should by no means rate as high as he in character or essential attainment.

In this process, it is curious that, while I was discovering him and beginning to like him, he was also discovering me and, I have every evidence, beginning to like me. Several times he has gone out of his busy way to do me little unostentatious favors which I know well he would not do for everybody. This is a pleasure to me.

June 7. Twenty-fourth day. I am still improving, but with anxious reminders of the old pain. . . . It may be only transitory.

"Why," asked my agreeable nurse, "do you write so much?"

"Why," said I, "because I enjoy it."

I could see that she was not fully satisfied with my reply. How could anyone enjoy writing?

I have been thinking of it as I lie here with my notebooks on the little bed table. Why do I write?—I can think of no better reply than the one I made to my nurse. I have really no better reason.

I write what I am, what I think, what I feel. Such and such an unashamed human being! Will anyone ever read what I have written? Who knows? If I had tried to

write what I thought other people thought, or felt, if I
had tried to write what I thought they would like and
pay for, I should have failed utterly—and died of bore-
dom. As it is, I have had the primary reward, and that
the richest; I have discovered myself; I have enjoyed my
own mind. If, afterward, anyone cares, I shall be glad.
It will all be clear profit. If no one cares, well and good,
I have had my pleasure of it.

I found a passage the other day in Lewes' *Life of
Goethe*, in a letter written by Schiller, which has an
application, perhaps a little dim, to what I have just
said:

"So soon as a man lets me see that there is anything
in poetical representations that interest him more than
internal necessity and truth, I give him up."

Quite a list of visitors today. I am learning to take
them as they are—with their hospital manners—I find I
like them better.

What pleasant half hours and hours have I spent,
these last weeks, thinking how best to say a thought. A
painter must have his paints and his brushes; a musi-
cian, his instrument; how favored then the writer who
can lie back among his pillows and arrange words that
are already stored in his mind, creating out of their infinite variety new patterns to delight him. To say a thing

and see it! To search for a word among the dusty store, or better yet, to *feel* for one—to place it here or fit it there, so that the content of a thought may appear with new beauty or greater power. To satisfy *oneself!*

Many and many a time the search for a more exact or a more beautiful word actually helps to proliferate the thought or enlarge the emotion. In the heat of writing there come flying to the tip of the pen—who knows by what magic?—refinements, significances, analogies that one did not dream he ever knew.

4. ESCAPE

JUNE 8. Twenty-fifth day. Fog and clouds and cool damp airs stirring the leaves at my window. I had a hard night with much pain, and while I am easier this morning, I think I have been too sanguine. The doctor, however, was in to reassure me. It is something to be able to sit up—partly sit up.

Speaking of reading, I have likewise escaped temporarily the tyranny of a strictly prescribed and dominating subject. Oh, I know well the enrichment that comes of saturation in one minute angle of life—to know everything about something!—and I know well, also, the intellectual fascination of it, and finally the sense of confidence and security, the kind of knowledge that is also a kind of character. Such innumerable volumes have I read relating to the life and times of Woodrow Wilson, such ton-loads—literally, I think, thousands—of documents, reports, letters, digests! I regret none of it.

I have not, it is true, been without my deeply prized bed books in wider fields—I am never without them—but there has been in these days of my illness, a new and peculiar delight in utter desultoriness!—looking in where I please, through unfamiliar peepholes, at this astonishing world. It has seemed not to matter much—I was so hungry—what book I served myself. Every last one of them, good or bad, has somehow pleased my appetite, has given me something I wanted, or something I enjoyed, at least a springboard for new thought.

I have been rereading Trollope's novels—good roast-beef British, with a hearty, healthy, honest, commonplace soul within them. Books without skepticism, if with the sturdy contempt of a free spirit, expressing itself in irony, when it considers the hypocrisies of society. But of real doubt there is not a trace: there was never a writer surer of his standards of what was right and what seemly. I found little worth remembering, at least verbally. This lighted passage in *Barchester Towers:* "She well knew the great architectural secret of decorating her constructions and never descended to construct a decoration."

This reading of the novels led me to recall a long-cherished curiosity to look into Trollope's *Autobiography,* and so I sent out and got it. Why haven't I had it before? If I had, I should have missed during this illness a wholly amusing, delightful, and illuminating experience. It makes me newly hopeful that there may be many another book, such as this, that I have yet to see as the swift years roll by. I think it worth all of Trollope's novels put together. I don't know where one could find a more perfect living picture of the Victorian Englishman at his sturdy best than in this book, as innocent of duplicity as a child, a marvel of square-toed certainty, a pattern of earnest self-discipline. In his novels, a few of his characters come vigorously to life, but even at their best they are shadowy indeed compared with the forthright Britisher who marches through this autobiography. One wonders, reading the narrative of his bitter boyhood, how he ever became the man of character he was, still more, considering his neglected education, the triumphant writer. One wonders, of all things, how, with his limitations—of which poverty, in the earlier years, was not the least—he became such a devoted horseman, loving beyond anything else the sport of riding to the hounds, full-clad in red coat and russet breeches. He wonders himself, says he cannot understand it or explain it. It is indeed a signatory of his life, a symbol of his achievement. He is too heavy to ride well, and sometimes mounts his horse, which must be strong and sure to carry him, by "getting on a bank" —but he rides. He is half-blind, frequently does not see the hounds at all, much less the fox—but he rides! Often he does not see the fences when he comes to them—or the ditches—or the bogs—but he jumps! If he lands head first, he is soon up again, riding after other foxes he never sees, jumping other fences he does not know are there. And all with what glorious, obstinate, exhilarating vigor! A classic Britisher, in the full flowering of Victorian certainties, here presenting himself for the delectation of coming generations! How I have enjoyed the book. As for the picture of honest, hard-toiling, commonsense carpentry in literature—with the record of wages meticulously set down, is there anything like it anywhere in any language? (I have not read Arnold Bennett's diary, which bears, I hear, some similarity in this regard—and I don't intend to.) Was there ever in the world a writer who, in the course of a life devoted busily to public office, turned off such an enormous number of first-rate second-rate books?

JUNE 9. Twenty-sixth day. Another fine spring day. I am actually sitting up to write this!

"You will be glad, I think," said the nurse, "to be getting home again."

"Yes," said I, answering as she expected, "I shall be glad to be getting home again."

In reality I have not been freer than I have been here in this room; scarcely, I think, happier, in spite of periods of tormenting pain, and weakness and weariness, for many a long month. I shall indeed go back to my hillside with joy—the tall white foxgloves, I am told, are in stately bloom—I shall be namelessly glad to see the great apple trees in my orchard and hear the busy hum of my bees. Friends and family I shall be eager to see. I shall be soberly satisfied to find my familiar place among all the trivial, normal, necessary things of life. But sitting here this morning languorously, languorously, the real tasks of my life seem Mount Everests of inaccessibility. The deadly monsoon I can hear roaring, wild blasts, and the dreadful avalanche!

JUNE 10. Twenty-seventh day. Time does count: I am really gaining strength. It just occurs to me, this morning, as something quite new and a little surprising: I am still alive. I may still be able to work! I may still stand up among men as one to be reckoned with! It is a suddenly joyous sensation. But the doctors remain reticent in their prophecies. . . .

A little desultory reading. Hazlitt's *Essays*, more of Lewes' *Goethe*. I have finished *Mansfield Park;* what a comedown from *Pride and Prejudice!* There is indeed a skill in detail, a deftness in handling incidents, that is wanting in the earlier book, for by 1816 Miss Austen had written many volumes, but the magic of genius, the magnificent energy of attack, the transmutation of words into actual life are not there. Nor are the characters so sharply defined, though there are realizations that in another author would be highly praised, but the condensation—the *rush*—of the story is not there. It seems to hang upon ideas rather than emotion, and toward the end drags heavily.

JUNE 11. Twenty-eighth day. I had a hard night, tormented with pain. Not so severe as in the early part of my captivity—bad enough. I have not seen the doctors yet this morning, but any hope I may have had of getting home soon has gone glimmering.

It was a blessing to see J. and other friends.

I have been restless. . . .

When I first got up the other day, I looked in the mirror.

"But," I said, "they don't know what I have inside me."

Well, we have to live with what we look like, this whether we are ill or well; and I never yet found any human being who was wholly satisfied. Years ago I knew a fine woman who had the most glorious of glowing dark eyes, the crown of her beauty; she told me that one of the bitter sorrows of her teens was that she did not have blue eyes.

Several times in my life I have had the sense of having lived this moment once before, so convincing that I know, or think I know, what will happen next, and what I shall think, feel, say. . . .

As to a certain friendship, I thought ruefully that, in being a friend, I had not been *enough* of a friend. Loving, I had not loved *enough*. Long afterward I thought this.

Every nurse ought, while in training, to have a required course in illness. Say a mandatory appendix! It would improve some I know.

I have come a long way and would not turn back. Beyond the next hill, a turn or two, through a forest, past a plain, I shall come at length, quite weary I think, to my Inn. And I shall sleep well there; I shall sleep long and well.

June 12. I am considerably better, but weary. Yesterday I can see I was low in my mind—rare for me. It takes all there is in a man to come through such experiences as I have been having. They leave him exhausted in spirit as well as in body.

In some ways—I am almost ashamed to say it—I am regretful to have to leave this place; there are so many interesting things to think about, and so little interruption in doing it.

June 13. Thirtieth day. A chill dark day with lowering clouds. I am much more hopeful; I seem now to be really on the upgrade. I slept easily most of the night, and if somewhat weary this morning, my mind is tranquil. Reading Charles Dickens' letters; not much for me. Also a highly suggestive book on Sweden called *The Middle Way*, which sets forth a method for the orderly and gradual solution of some of the vast problems now confronting the world, involving the slow breakdown of the old capitalistic system. It reveals a *modus vivendi* for escaping either revolutionary extreme, with the attendant social and political catastrophes, of Bolshevism and Fascism. It is just the method I have been hoping against hope would develop more actively in this country. The vital inner spark is the spontaneous popular growth of producers' and consumers' co-operation in all of their forms. But there is never any short-cut to the land of promise. . . .

So many things I don't know, so many I am not sure about, and must say so. I have been instructed by the Elders regarding some of these things, but did the Elders know? I am not at all sure about the Elders.

JUNE 14. Another dour morning with grim skies and a slow rain falling. It is the thirty-first day of my captivity, better than the twenty-ninth, and better far than the twentieth. I know I must be recovering by one homely sign: I have not so enjoyed a breakfast in many a month as I did this morning, sitting up luxuriously in bed, sipping my coffee. Two little brown sausages grilled to absolute perfection brought in to me by an agreeable and smiling young nurse, and eaten with my eggs and toast, I shall not soon forget—a veritable symphony! It is likely now that I shall be released within a day or so. J. came at noon, and other friends. I delighted in the visit and the talk.

How much of our content in life is due to such simple things as well-browned sausages!

I met a man the other day in this hospital who delivered himself to me complete in about ten minutes. He is like one of the old folk tunes: a single little theme, good and pleasant to the ear. A simple tune one likes and would be glad to hear again; but if I were to be with him a year there would, I think, be nothing more: the same little theme, the same little pipe of his personality. I like him: a good man, recently retired on a pension after years of devoted and loyal service. A good husband I hear; a good father; a good citizen, no doubt, so far as he goes. But he can only repeat himself, nor ever improvise; there are millions of him in the bony framework of this nation!

As I have said before, I have positively enjoyed much of my experience in this hospital, and yet the intimate sights, sounds, actions, facts, relating to one's physical life, the intense concentration upon them, so overwhelming in a hospital, soon begin to wear upon the

spirit of man. I should think fine natures here continu-
ously occupied—and there is scarcely nobler work anywhere to be found—would need often to seek out a
mountaintop or walk, some clear night, under the stars.
I have been here now for a month, to my vast benefit. I
admire profoundly what is being done here, the skill of
the physicians, the agreeable and intelligent service of
the nurses—I am grateful for what I have myself received in healing attention—but I have had moments of
intense longing to be free of this concentrated and intimate consideration of the body. I long to walk down
through my own orchard. I long to stand and listen to
the busy hum of my bees; I long to look off across my
meadow to the everlasting hills. Not so much for these
things in themselves I long, but for what they mean to
me. For I want the mysterious things of the Heights and
the Depths. I want the glory of that something which is
above and beyond the human body where I live. I want
a Voice I know, but cannot clearly hear; a Vision I
cannot wholly see. I want to know that which I can
never know, which is of perfect beauty; I long for that
which is everlasting and eternal.

I find myself often wishing to speak of God. All that
I long for most, all that is best in me at my best, all that I
know and feel with the deepest passion of my being, is
contained in my idea of God. But when I speak to another of God, it is his idea of God that he straightway
thinks of, and we can by no means understand each

other. There were old sects that knew Him only as the Nameless One, He Who Could Not Be Expressed, who *Was,* but was not Named. Something I have of the feeling of those old anchorites! Once I try to bound Him, He eludes me; but walking of an evening in my garden, quiet there, I find Him often near.

Poor people, poor people, trying to entangle God in a loop of weak words, confine him in their own finitude where, like some Samson, he may make himself serviceable by grinding their little grists of corn.

I know one sect that will be going to God every morning for advice in their petty daily doings, whether they shall dine at two, and travel to New York at four. How discouraged the Creator must be that he has, after all, created only children. Running to him every time they stub their toes! Willing to dare nothing themselves, expecting Him to think for them and act for them at every turn.

I recall vividly the wondering shame I felt as a youth listening to a church full of pretty good human beings mournfully singing from the old hymnbook:

> *Oh to be nothing, nothing,*
> *Only to lie at His feet.*

In my inmost thought, even at that time, I rejected utterly any God who would demand, much less accept, such a groveling offer of "broken and emptied vessels."

As a father, I should be irritated with a son who could

not or would not take his life into his own hands, do his own hard thinking, make his own mistakes, and in the end add to my pride by creating something himself out of the void. How discouraged the Creator must be—if it were possible to discourage an Intelligence that was all-knowing—if he has failed to produce, here and there, a grown-up man! Looking about, sometimes, I think He must veritably have moments when the human race looks to Him, after all, a somewhat dubious experiment.

In this connection I have just run across a quotation from Lessing that is apropos: "If God would give me the truth, I would decline the gift, preferring the labor of seeking it for myself." I find this in Eckermann's *Conversations with Goethe,* which I am now reading.

Do I contradict myself? Very well then, I contradict myself! Do I grope for intangible things? Very well, then, being what I am, I grope for intangible things. Nothing that I see finally satisfies me; I have far yet to go. I think the only thing really worth noting about me is that which will not be satisfied. I am most interesting where I am most insatiable.

JUNE 15. Thirty-second day. Still dark, with a thin rain coming straight down. It does not depress me. I think of my garden and orchard. It looks now as though I should be going home tomorrow, and I have been glancing back over what I have written since I came here. I am amazed at the sheer number of pages of white paper despoiled, considering how little, during many of those miserable days, I could do. Some 20,000 words, roughly estimated, enough for a slim book if the printer would be kind and use large type. What a hodgepodge! Everything from the sublime to the ridiculous!

And yet, as I think of it, how like a man's mind. I have turned it out, since I enjoy nothing in this world so much as writing, just as it came to me: the things I happened at the moment to be thinking about, not at all considering whether they were things I ought to say, or whether the saying of them could be of any possible use afterward, to me or to anyone else. The saying was enough: it eased me, it released me, it occupied weary half hours—in short, it delighted me.

I was about to say that I turned out my mind completely, as an old lady might turn out her rag bag when she considers piecing a quilt; but as I think of it, I am even more astonished by what I have not said than by what I have. It would have been well perhaps if I had been as wise as the old lady and considered a quilt in the first place. I could then have chosen well my pieces and, by dint of a little provident labor, made something really sensible and practical that would in future chilly evenings (after I have paid these doctors' bills) keep me warm. I did nothing of the sort; I wrote when I liked, what came most spontaneously at the moment into my mind. And naturally, I left out all of the most

important things in the world, judging at least by the
headlines in the newspapers—many things in which I
have, or have had, these many years, a keen interest.
While I have been lying here, the Republicans have
met at Chicago and nominated a candidate for the
Presidency; next week the Democrats will nominate
theirs. I know quite well who they are to be; I am not
stirred. Does it really make much difference, considering
"all that human hearts endure," which is elected? I read
the dispatches which are intended to whip up public
excitement; I yawn and turn over.

I know that Europe is in process of dissolution, that
any day there may be upheavals that will shake the
world. I remain calm. Since 1914 I have been shocked
by such a number of crises! I saw such carnage in 1918,
and so many catastrophes since, that my capacity for
horror and fear seems benumbed. My mind turns irre-
sistably to the bobolinks I can see from my window, lifting and singing above the meadow grass. I can look at
them long and be content. I agree entirely with Goethe,
whose life by Lewes I have been reading, who was so
little stirred by the battles of the French Revolution that
he spent his time while the cannon were literally roaring around him "dictating to Vagel a loose sketch of my
theory [of color]." He is in such ecstasies over the
"optical phenomena observed in the water" that he pays
no attention to the bombardment of Verdun; but it does
concern him that he cannot keep his notebooks dry. I

forget, also, that there is war in China—there always is!
—and I pass over with scarcely more than a cursory
glance the distressful news that a million human beings
are starving there. It may be a sad defect, but I am little
given to statistical suffering. One poor Chinese laundry-
man known to me, suffering in the next street, would
cause me more anxiety than the million in China: for
the one I could possibly help, the million are beyond
me. I am aware of blustering and braggadocio in Italy—
ever since Mussolini was successful in robbing the
miserable Ethiopians, after slaughtering as many as
possible, of all they possessed. And I cannot forget that
there are mighty things going on within Germany and
Russia, so mighty and so complex that they stagger and
distress my understanding. I see also that there is a man
in America who proposes to convert our people to broth-
erly love before the election next November. Ho hum!
Ho hum! I think I am something like the "ancient
people" that the old Chinese philosopher tells about—I
find the account in Lin Yutang's excellent book—who
"were not compelled to say anything," but "suddenly
they said something purely of their own accord." And
having done this supremely wise thing, and "having
finished what they had to say, they took leave and de-
parted."

And so, writing purely of my own accord, of things I
was at the moment most delighted in, and having finished what I had to say, I take leave and depart.

The Last Thing of All

XV

The Last Thing of All

NOT LONG AGO my eye chanced to fall on these
lines:

So much do I love wandering,
So much I love the sea and sky,
That it will be a piteous thing
In one small grave to lie.
—Zoë Akins, *The Wanderer*

For a brief moment these wistful words struck me to
the heart, since they expressed a thought that I too, in
certain moods, have sometimes had. But it was only for
a moment, for I recalled, quite unexpectedly, a passage
from old robust Montaigne that had long lain quiet in
my mind:

"Let death take me," said he, "while I am planting
my cabbages—indifferent to him and still more indifferent to my unfinished garden."

"That," said I to myself, "is how I myself should like well to feel."

A little later, I came upon an incident that pleased me even better. It concerned a noble American who left us not so long ago. I mean Oliver Wendell Holmes, the jurist. When he was dying, at the age of 94, a friend came in with pity in his eyes to see him. The smiling old man, lying there, responded by thumbing his nose.

"To die," as Walt Whitman says, "is different from what anyone supposed—and luckier."

For Mary Stafford Whiting
who is carrying on the tradition
of Oliver Wendell Holmes
                    --August, 1986

David Grayson was the pen name of accomplished turn of the century journalist Ray Stannard Baker. From the March day in 1894 when Baker set out to follow Coxey's Army for the Chicago *Record*, he became an American chronicler. "When I really enjoyed an experience, when I saw or heard something which struck me as wonderful, when I met a man or a woman who interested me, whom I deeply admired or loved, I could not let these things go by with a glance...Of all the ways ever I found for squeezing the last savor from an experience, the best is to write about it..."

Baker had a long, productive relationship with the prestigious *McClure's Magazine*, bringing to its pages portraits of some of the day's geniuses: Theodore Roosevelt, Joel Chandler Harris, Stephen Crane, Admiral Dewey, Thomas Alva Edison, Guglielmo Marconi... At a political gathering in January, 1910, he was enlightened with a speech by the president of Princeton University. "Here, it seemed, was the magical touch of great leadership: the touch of courage. Was (this man) after all really available as a national leader?" Thus began the close friendship of Ray Stannard Baker and Woodrow Wilson, Baker following the future president throughout his administration and ultimately to Europe in 1918, where he organized the press department at the Paris Peace Conference and reported the long, often bitter controversies over the League of Nations. Baker became Woodrow Wilson's official biographer and was awarded the Pulitzer Prize for his seven-volume *Woodrow Wilson: Life and Letters.*

But Ray Stannard Baker was a lover of quiet ways and simple pleasures, goals not easily attained in the hectic journalistic world. Thus emerged David Grayson, the writer in Baker who "wished most, if it can be expressed in a phrase, to be an introducer of human beings to one another, to be a maker of understandings." In pursuit of a more rational lifestyle, he moved his family to Amherst, Massachusetts, where they built their quiet, country dream home. "Every tree, every shrub, every berry bush around the house and in the garden we planted with our own hands." From his Amherst refuge, Grayson recorded his daily thoughts and observations on the state of the farm, his neighbors, his bees, the nation and mankind.